Talking Heads

Talking Heads

Alan Bennett

BBC
BOOKS

A Woman of No Importance was first published by BBC Books
in *Objects of Affection* in 1982. © Forelake Ltd 1982
A Chip in the Sugar, *Bed Among the Lentils*, *A Lady of Letters*, *Her Big Chance*,
Soldiering On and *A Cream Cracker Under the Settee* were first published by BBC
Books in *Talking Heads* in 1988. © Forelake Ltd 1988
The Hand of God, *Miss Fozzard Finds Her Feet*, *Playing Sandwiches*, *The Outside
Dog*, *Nights in the Gardens of Spain* and *Waiting for the Telegram* were first
published by BBC Books in *Talking Heads 2* in 1998. © Forelake Ltd 1998

11

This edition published in 2007 by BBC Books, an imprint of Ebury Publishing.
A Random House Group company.
First published in hardback 1998. Published in paperback in 2001.

The Random House Group Limited Reg. No. 954009
Addresses for companies within the Random House Group can be found at
www.randomhouse.co.uk

Commissioning Editors: Vivien Bowler and Martin Redfern
Project Editor: Martha Caute
Designer: Linda Blakemore

ISBN 978 1846 072 598

Printed and bound in Great Britain by Clays Ltd, St Ives plc

CONTENTS

Introduction 9

A WOMAN OF NO IMPORTANCE 15

Introduction to Talking Heads 39

A CHIP IN THE SUGAR 51

BED AMONG THE LENTILS 69

A LADY OF LETTERS 87

HER BIG CHANCE 103

SOLDIERING ON 123

A CREAM CRACKER UNDER THE SETTEE 139

Introduction to Talking Heads 2 155

THE HAND OF GOD 177

MISS FOZZARD FINDS HER FEET 191

PLAYING SANDWICHES 209

THE OUTSIDE DOG 225

NIGHTS IN THE GARDENS OF SPAIN 239

WAITING FOR THE TELEGRAM 255

In memory of

INNES LLOYD

1925–1991

INTRODUCTION

This collection includes the first and second series of *Talking Heads*, twelve monologues in all, together with the introductions I wrote for each series. However, it seems appropriate to include with them an earlier monologue, *A Woman of No Importance*, which was first televised in 1982 and for which I did this introduction.

> I wrote *A Woman of No Importance* thinking I might direct it myself. I have never directed either for the stage or television and the possibility of having to do so accounts for the simplicity (not to say crudity) of the form: the piece is for one actress, who speaks directly to camera.
>
> Thinking I would be able to manage at the most two cameras, I planned the play as a series of midshots with the camera tracking in very slowly to a close-up, holding the close-up for a while then, just as slowly, coming out again. I didn't figure on there being any cuts within scenes, though this would place a heavy burden on the performer, some sections being pretty lengthy: the first speech, for instance lasts twelve minutes. To shoot in such a way makes cutting virtually impossible: one fluff, and it's back to the top of the scene again. Autocue is one answer, but Patricia Routledge, for whom the piece was written, was anxious to avoid this, and quite rightly. Even

when a performer is in full command of the text, the sight of it slowly reeling down over the camera lens exercises an hypnotic effect, and an element of the rabbit fascinated by the snake enters in. I therefore planned on using a second camera, shooting Miss Schofield in profile. This would provide a shot to which one could cut if it proved necessary to do so.

In the event, because I was working on one of the other plays, I didn't direct the piece, which was done by Giles Foster. He adhered faithfully to the form I'd given the play, though to begin with finding the restrictions it imposed irksome and unnerving. He began by moving the play around, with Miss Schofield traversing the studio to match the movements described in the text. Rehearsal was a process of simplification whereby these movements were taken back inside the character, who ended up static in front of the camera as I had originally imagined. There are in fact some cuts within sections, when a gesture or slight turn of the head make it possible to switch to a slightly different shot without being false to the fairly relentless nature of the piece. Of course such directness and simplicity may not be thought to work. 'Talking heads' is a synonym in television for boredom, and here is just one head, not two. And Miss Schofield is a bore. But to have her in full close-up, retailing in unremitting detail how she borrowed the salt in the canteen takes one, I hope, beyond tedium.

The first few lines of the play are poached. In the Festival of Britain, which I visited as a boy, there was a pavilion (I suspect I might be irritated by it now) called The Lion and the Unicorn, devoted to Englishness. It included a console where, by pressing a button, one heard

> snatches of typical English conversation. These had been written by (I think) Stephen Potter and were performed by Joyce Grenfell. One in particular concerned a disaster that befell a middle-class lady, and began: 'I was perfectly all right on the Monday. I was perfectly all right on the Tuesday. I was perfectly all right on the Wednesday. I was perfectly all right on the Thursday until lunchtime, when I just ate a little poached salmon: five minutes later I was *rolling about the floor*.'

With the experience accumulated from the later monologues there are other observations I can add about the technique appropriate for their presentation. The more still (and even static) the speaker is the better the monologue works. However much the text might seem to demand it too much movement dissipates interest and raises awkward questions, chief among them, 'Whom does this person think they're talking to?' Whereas if the speaker is relatively still and the camera has them in a medium to close shot such questions do not arise. I don't know why this should be but it is so.

There are also certain patterns in the form which, to begin with, I was unaware of but which I now see are essential to the action – and for all that there is just one person talking there is quite a bit of action. A section will often end with a seemingly throwaway remark that carries the plot forward: Violet's remarks about Francis at the end of several of the sections of *Waiting for the Telegram* chart his separate decline; in *The Outside Dog* Marjory's, 'He seems to have lost another anorak, this one fur-lined,' strikes the first note of unease about her murderous husband; and in *Playing Sandwiches* Wilfred's 'On my way home I called in at the sweet shop,' alerts the audience to the fact that something dreadful is about to happen. And, of course, by the beginning of the next section it has happened as the action of these stories generally takes place in the intervals between sections, what has happened recalled by the speaker rather than narrated as it occurs.

It would be quite possible to tell these stories in a different (and a more conventional) way, a question that will be found in the introduction to the first *Talking Heads* series.

A WOMAN OF NO IMPORTANCE

Peggy · Patricia Routledge

PEGGY IS A MIDDLE-AGED WOMAN. SHE TALKS DIRECTLY TO CAMERA AGAINST A NEUTRAL BACKGROUND.

I was all right on the Monday. I was all right on the Tuesday. And I was all right on the Wednesday until lunchtime, at which point all my nice little routine went out of the window.

Normally, i.e. provided Miss Hayman isn't paying us one of her state visits, come half past twelve and I'm ready to down tools and call it a morning. I put on a lick of paint, slip over and spend a penny in Costing...I should technically use the one in Records but I've told them, that lavatory seat is a death trap. And I'm not ringing up again. 'Try a bit of sellotape.' What are they paid for? I'll then rout out Miss Brunskill from 402 and we'll meander gently over for our midday meal. But you just have to hit it right because, give it another five minutes, and believe me that canteen is dog eat dog.

However if you can manage to nip in before the avalanche you have the pick of the tables and there's still some semblance of hygiene. Our particular stamping ground is just the other side of the bamboo framework thing they tried to grow ivy up. It's what Miss Brunskill calls 'our little backwater'. We're more or less fixtures there and have been for yonks. In fact Mr Skidmore came by with his tray last week just as we were concluding our coffee and he said, 'Well, girls. Fancy seeing you!' We laughed. Girls! Mr Skidmore generally gravitates to the table in the far corner under that silly productivity thermometer-type thing. 'Export or Die'. It's actually broken – stuck anyway – but it's where management tend to foregather since we've had this absurd 'All Barriers Down' policy. Once upon a time management had tables roped off. That's gone, only they still congregate there. 'Huddling together for warmth,' Mr Rudyard calls it. I said to Mr Cresswell, 'You can tell who's an activist.' We laughed, because anybody more conformist than Mr Rudyard you couldn't want, and he has beautiful fingernails. Of course once the management started frequenting that particular table sure enough Miss Hayman and the Personnel brigade pitch camp next door. And she'll turn around and chat to Mr Skidmore over the back of her chair. She never used to have all that hair.

Our table though we're very much the happy family. There's me, Miss Brunskill, Mr Cresswell and Mr Rudyard, Pauline Lucas, who's ex-Projects...to tell the truth she's still Projects, only she's in Presentation wearing her Projects hat. Then there's Trish Trotter (when she's not in one of her 'bit of cheese and an apple' phases); Joy Pedley pays us the occasional visit, but by and large that's the hard core. Trish Trotter is the only one with a right weight problem but we're all salad fanatics and keep one another in line. I have to watch my stomach anyway and salad suits Miss Brunskill because she's a big Christian Scientist. But to add that bit of excitement I bring along some of my home-made French dressing. Mr Cresswell keeps pestering me to give Mr Rudyard what he calls 'the secret formula'. He's a keen cook, Mr Rudyard. Little moustache, back like a ramrod, you'd never guess it. I pretend there's a mystery ingredient and won't let on. We laugh.

People are a bit envious of us, I know. I ran into Mr McCorquodale the other day when we were both queueing in (guess!) Accounts and he said, 'You do seem to have a good time at your table, Peggy. What do you talk about?' And I didn't know. I mean, what do we talk about? Pauline's mother keeps getting a nasty rash that affects her elbows. We'd been discussing that. Mr Cresswell and Mr Rudyard were going in for some new curtains for their lounge and were debating about whether to have Thames Green. And I was saying if Thames Green was the green I thought it was I liked it in a front door but wasn't keen on it in curtains. So that made for some quite lively discussion. And Trish Trotter had got hold of some new gen on runner beans as part of a calorie-controlled diet, and we kicked that around for a bit. But honestly, that was all it was. I don't know what we do talk about half the time! My secret is, I don't talk about myself. When Joy Pedley went to Thirsk on a 'Know Your Client' course that was apparently the whole gist of it: concentrate on the other person. I said, 'Well, I've no need to go to Thirsk to learn that. It's something I've been born with.' We laughed.

Once we've lined up our eats and got the table organised Miss B. gets her nose into her crossword while I scan the horizon for the rest of the gang. I have to be on my toes because there's always some bright spark wanting to commandeer them and drag them off elsewhere. I don't think people like to see other people enjoying themselves, basically. Take Pauline Lucas. The other day, she came in with young Stuart Selby. He's ginger, and when Mr Oyston went up into Accounts and Mrs Ramaroop moved to Keighley, Stuart did a bit of a dog's hind leg and got into Costing. Him and Pauline were making a beeline for the window, which is in the Smoking area. Now Pauline doesn't smoke, in fact rather the reverse. So I sang out, 'You're not deserting us, are you Pauline? Fetch Stuart over here. See how the other half lives!' So she did. Only halfway he ran into Wendy Walsh and it ended up just being me and Pauline. I said to her, 'That was a narrow escape.' She said, 'Yes.' We laughed. Her acne's heaps better.

And then look at Mr Cresswell and Mr Rudyard. It's the

biggest wonder last week they didn't get sat with the truck drivers. They were dawdling past with their trays and there was room but luckily I just happened to be going by en route for some coffee and saw which way the wind was blowing and rescued them in the nick of time. They were so grateful. I said 'You two! You don't know you're born!' They laughed.

However, as I say, on this particular Wednesday I'm in the office, it's half past twelve and I'm just thinking, 'Time you were getting your skates on, Peggy,' when suddenly the door opens and nobody comes in. I didn't even look up. I just said, 'Yes, Mr Slattery?' He was on his hands and knees with a pro forma in his mouth. Anybody else would have got up. Not him. He crawls up to me, pretending to be a dog and starts begging, this bit of paper in his mouth! I thought, 'You're a grown man. You've got a son at catering college; your wife's in and out of mental hospital and you're begging like a dog.' I enjoy a joke, but I didn't laugh.

Surprise, surprise he's after a favour. The bit of paper is the Squash Ladder. Would I run him off two dozen copies? I said, 'Yes. By all means. At two o'clock.' He said, 'No. Now.' Wants to put them round in the lunch hour. I said, 'Sorry. No can do.' I haven't forgotten the works outing. Running round with that thing on his head. He was like a crazed animal. I said, 'Anybody with an atom of consideration would have come down earlier. Squash Ladder! It's half past twelve.' He said, 'It's not for me.' I said 'Who's it for?' He said, 'Mr Skidmore.'

Pause.

Well, as luck would have it I hadn't actually switched the machine off. And, knowing Trevor Slattery, Mr Skidmore had probably asked him to do it first thing and he'd only just got round to it. I know Mr Skidmore: courtesy is his middle name. But it did mean I didn't get out of the office until twenty to, by which time of course there's no Miss Brunskill. Any delay and La Brunskill's off like a shot from a gun, plastic hip or no plastic hip.

By this time of course the canteen is chock-a-block. I was five minutes just getting inside the door, and if I'd waited for a please or thank you I'd be stood there yet. They looked to be about to introduce martial law round the salad bowl so I thought, 'Little adventure, I'll opt for the hot dish of the day, steak bits or chicken pieces.' I knew the woman doling it out because she gets on the 56. She's black but I take people as they come, and seeing it was me she scrapes me up the last of the steak bits. I topped it off with some mushrooms, and trust me if I didn't get the last of the yogurts as well. I heard somebody behind me say 'Damn'. I laughed.

I beetled over to our table but no Pauline, no Mr Cresswell and no Mr Rudyard. It's a cast of unknowns and only Miss Brunskill that I recognise. I said, 'Didn't you save me a place?' She said, 'I thought you'd been and gone.' Been and gone? How could I have been and gone, she knows I'm meticulous. But I just said, 'Oh' rather pointedly, and started touring round.

Eventually I pinpoint Pauline sat with little Stuart Selby, only there's no room there either. 'Scattered to the four winds today, Pauline,' I said. 'Yes,' she said, and he laughed. I see she's starting another spot.

I trek over to the far side and blow me if Mr Cresswell and Mr Rudyard aren't sat with all the maintenance men, some of them still in their overalls. Mr Cresswell is smoking between courses, something he never does with us, a treacle sponge just stuck there, waiting. Mr Rudyard is having a salad and I wave my jar of French dressing in case he wants some but he doesn't see me because for some reason he's not wearing his glasses.

Just then I spot somebody vacating a place up at the top end. I say, 'Room for a little one?' only nobody takes on. They're young, mostly from Design, moustaches and those little T-shirty things, having some silly conversation about a topless Tandoori restaurant. I start on my steak bits, only to find that what she's given me is mainly gristle. I don't suppose they distinguish in Jamaica. I thought, 'Well, I'll have a little salt, perk it up a bit,' but as luck would have it there's none on the table, so I get up again and go in quest of some. The first salt I spot is on the table opposite, which happens to be the table patronised by the management; and who should be sat there but Mr Skidmore. So I asked him if I could borrow their salt. 'Excuse me, Mr Skidmore,' was what I said, 'but could I relieve you temporarily of your salt?' I saw Miss Hayman's head come round. She'd naturally think I was crawling. I wasn't. I just wanted some salt. Anyway, Mr Skidmore was very obliging. 'By all means,' he said. 'Would you like the pepper too?' I said, 'That's most civil of you, but I'm not a big pepper fan.' So I just took the salt, put a bit on the side of my plate and took it back. 'Much obliged,' I said. 'Don't mention it,' Mr Skidmore said. 'Any time.' He has impeccable manners, they have a big detached house at Alwoodley, his wife has had a nervous breakdown, wears one of those sheepskin coats.

I suddenly bethought me of the Squash Ladder, so just after I'd replaced the salt I said, 'Oh, by the way, I ran you off those copies of the Squash Ladder,' not in a loud voice, just person to person. He said, 'What?' I said, 'I ran you off those copies of the Squash Ladder.' He said, 'Squash Ladder?' I said, 'Yes.' He said, 'Not my pigeon.' I said, 'Why?' He said, 'Didn't you know? There's been a flare-up with my hernia.' Well I didn't know. I can't see how I would be expected to know. Somebody laughed. I said, 'Oh, I am sorry.' He said, 'I'm not. Blessing in disguise. Squash is Slattery's pigeon now.'

I went back to my table and sat down. I felt really sickened. He'd done it on me had Mr Slattery.

After a bit Trish Trotter rolls up and parks herself next to me. She says, 'Are you not eating your steak bits?' I said, 'No.' She said, 'Don't mind if I do,' and helps herself. She shouldn't wear trousers.

Anyway it was that afternoon that I first began to feel really off it. I went home at half past four.

FADE QUICKLY TO BLACK. *Still shot of her desk: very neat. A single flower in a glass. Typewriter with its cover on.*

I want the tableaux between scenes to look like still life paintings.

Peggy is now sat against another neutral background, wallpaper possibly – something to indicate she is at home.

I don't run to the doctor every five minutes. On the last occasion Dr Copeland sat me down and said, 'Miss Schofield. If I saw my other patients as seldom as I see you I should be out of business.' We laughed.

He's always pleased to see me: gets up when I come into the room, sits me down, then we converse about general topics for a minute or two before getting down to the nub of the matter. He has a picture of his children on the desk, taken years ago because the son's gone to Canada now and his daughter's an expert in man-made fibres. He never mentions his wife, I think she left him, he has a sensitive face. Cactuses seem to be his sideline. There's always one on his desk and he has a Cactus Calendar hung up. This month's was somewhere in Arizona, huge, a man stood beside it, tiny. I looked at it while he was diddling his hands after the previous patient.

There was a young man in the room and Dr Copeland introduced me. He said, 'This is Miss…' (he was looking at my notes) 'Miss Schofield. Mr Metcalf is a medical student; he's mistaken enough to want to become a doctor.' We laughed, but the boy kept a straight face. He had on one of those zip-up cardigans I think are a bit common so that didn't inspire confidence. Dr Copeland said would I object to Mr Metcalf conducting the examination provided he was standing by to see I came to no actual physical harm? We both laughed but Mr Metcalf was scratching a mark he'd found on the knee of his trousers.

Dr Copeland put him in the picture about me first: 'Miss Schofield has been coming to me over a period of twelve years. Her health is generally good, wouldn't you say, Miss Schofield?' – and he was going on, but I interjected. I said, 'Well, it is good,' I said, 'but it's quite likely to seem better than it is because I don't come running down to the surgery with every slightest thing.' 'Yes,' he said. 'If I saw my other patients as seldom as I see Miss Schofield I should be out of business.' He laughed. The student then asked me what the trouble was and I went through the saga of the steak bits and my subsequent tummy upset.

He said, 'Is there anything else beside that?' I said, 'No.' He said, 'Any problems at work?' I said, 'No.' He said, 'Any problems at home?' I said, 'No.' He said, 'You're single.' I said,

'Yes.' He said, 'Where are your parents?' I said, 'Mother's in her grave and father is in a Sunshine Home at Moortown.' He said, 'Do you feel bad about that?' (He didn't look more than seventeen.) I said, 'No. Not after the life he's lived.'

I saw him look at Dr Copeland, only he was toying with the calendar, sneaking a look at what next month's cactus was going to be. So this youth said, 'What life did he lead?' I said, 'A life that involved spending every other weekend at Carnforth with a blondified piece from the cosmetics counter at Timothy Whites and Taylors.' He said, 'Is that a shoe shop?' I said, 'You're thinking of Freeman, Hardy and Willis. It's a chemist. Or was. It's been taken over by Boots. And anyway she now has a little gown shop at Bispham. His previous was a Meltonian shoe cream demonstrator at Manfields, and what has this to do with my stomach?'

Dr Copeland said, 'Quite. I think it's about time you took an actual look at the patient, Metcalf.' So the young man examined me, the way they do pressing his hands into me and whatnot, and then calls over Dr Copeland to have a look. 'That's right,' I said. 'Make way for the expert.' Only neither of them laughed.

Dr Copeland kneaded me about a bit, but more profess-ionally and while he was washing his hands he said, 'Miss Schofield. I'm not in the least bit worried by your stomach. But, you being you, it wants looking at. There aren't many of us left!' We laughed. 'So just to be on the safe side I want to make an appointment for you to see a specialist, Mr Penry-Jones.' I said, 'Isn't his wife to do with the Music Festival?' He said, 'I don't know, is she?' I said, 'She is. I've seen a picture of her talking to Lord Harewood.' He took me to the door of the consulting room, which he doesn't do with everybody, and he took my hand (and I'm not a private patient). 'Thank you,' he said. 'Thank you for being a guinea pig.' We laughed. Only it's funny, just as I was coming out I saw the student's face and he was looking really pleased with himself.

She very slightly presses her hand into her stomach.

FADE TO BLACK AND UP AGAIN *to still shot of bedside table. Clock. Bedside lamp. A bottle of white medicine.*

FADE TO BLACK AND UP AGAIN: *Peggy is in a hospital bed.*

I've just had a shampoo and set. She's not done it too badly, bearing in mind she doesn't know my hair. Lois, her name is. She has a little salon. You go past Gyney, and it's smack opposite Maternity. It's a bit rudimentary, they just have it to perk up the morale of the pregnant mums basically, but, as Lois says, it's an open door policy just so long as you can find your way because this place is a rabbit warren. Lois said my hair was among the best she'd come across. It's the sort Italians make into wigs apparently, they have people scouring Europe for hair of this type. I should have had a perm last Tuesday only when Mr Penry-Jones whipped me in here it just went by the board.

Caused chaos at work. Miss Brunskill said after I'd rung up Mr McCorquodale and Mr Skidmore went into a huddle for fully half an hour and at the end of it they still couldn't figure out a way to work round me. In the finish Miss Hayman had to come down from the fifth floor – though not wearing her Personnel hat, thank God – and Pauline did her usual sideways jump from Records, but it's all a bit pass the parcel. Miss Brunskill says everybody is on their knees praying I come back soon.

I'd actually been feeling a lot better when I went along to see Mr Penry-Jones. He's got one of those big double-fronted houses in Park Square: vast rooms, wicked to heat. There was just one other woman in the waiting room, smartish, looked to have arthritis. I said, 'I wouldn't like this electricity bill,' but she just smiled. Then the housekeeper came and conducted me upstairs. I made some remark about it being spring but she didn't comment, a lot of them are Spanish these days. Mr Penry-Jones though was a very courtly oldish man, blue pin-striped suit, spotted bow-tie. I said, 'What a lovely fireplace.' He said, 'Yes. These are old houses.' I said, 'Georgian, I imagine.' 'Oh,' he said. 'I can see I'm in the presence of a connoisseur.' We laughed.

He examined me and I went through the story again, though I didn't actually mention the steak bits, and it was a beautiful carpet. Then he looked out of the window and asked me one or two questions about my bowels. I said, 'I believe your wife has a lot to do with the Music Festival.' He said, 'Yes.' I said, 'That must be very satisfying.' He says, 'Yes. It is. Last week she shook hands with the Queen.' I said, 'Well that's funny, because I stood as near to her as I am to you, at York in 1956. What an immaculate complexion!'

When I'd got dressed he said, 'Miss Schofield, you are a puzzle. I'm very intrigued.' I said, 'Oh?' He said, 'Have you got anything special on in the next couple of weeks?' he said. 'Because ideally what I would like to do is take you in, run a few tests and then go on from there. I'm absolutely certain there's nothing to get worked up about but we ought to have a little look. Is that all right?' I said, 'You're the doctor.' We laughed.

He made a point of coming downstairs with me. It was

just as some other doctor was helping the better-class-looking woman with arthritis into a car – it looked to be chauffeur driven. I went and sat on a seat in the square for a bit before I got the bus. The trees did look nice.

> GO TO BLACK AND UP AGAIN. *Miss Schofield is now sat by her hospital bed in a candlewick dressing gown.*

I've appointed myself newspaper lady. I go round first thing taking the orders for the papers, then I nip down and intercept the trolley on its way over. I said to Sister Tudor, 'Well, with a candlewick dressing gown I might as well.' Most of the others have these silly shorty things. Mine's more of a housecoat. The shade was called Careless Pink, only that's fifteen years ago. It's mostly the *Sun* or the *Mirror*, there's only two of us get the *Mail* and she's another Miss. I could tell straight away she was a bit more refined. Hysterectomy.

Of course I shan't be able to do the papers tomorrow because of my op.

When Princess Alexandra came round, this was the bed she stopped at, apparently.

I get on like a house on fire with the nurses. We do laugh. Nurse Trickett says I'm their star patient. She's little and a bit funny-looking but so goodhearted. 'How's our star patient?' she says. 'I hope you've been behaving yourself.' We laugh. She hasn't got a boy friend. I've promised to teach her shorthand typing. Her mother has gallstones, apparently. Nurse Gillis is the pretty one. I think she's just marking time till she finds the right man. And then there's Nurse Conkie, always smiling. I said to her, 'You're always smiling, you're a lesson to any shop steward, you.' She laughed and laughed the way they do when they're black.

Sister came in while she was laughing and said wasn't it time Mrs Boothman was turned over. She's all right is Sister, but she's like me: she has a lot on her plate. I said to her, 'I'm a professional woman myself.' She smiled.

Pause. Miss Schofield turns the name tag she has on her wrist.

Name on my wrist now: 'Schofield, Margaret, Miss.'

Pause.

Mr Penry-Jones comes round on a morning, and he fetches his students and they have to guess what's wrong. I said to Miss Brunskill, 'It's a bit of a game. If he doesn't know what the matter is, they won't.' He said, 'Gentlemen, a big question mark hangs over Miss Schofield's stomach.' They all laughed.

So tomorrow's the big day. He was telling the students what he's going to do. 'I'm just going to go in,' he said, 'and have a look round. We're not going to do anything, just a tour of inspection.' I chipped in, 'More of a guided tour, if all these are there.' They did laugh. Not Sister though. She can't afford to, I suppose. He's like a God to them, Mr Penry-Jones.

I do my bit here in different ways. I'm always going round the beds, having a word, particularly when someone isn't mobile. I run them little errands and tell the nurse if there's anything anybody's wanting. Mrs Maudsley opposite's on a drip and she was going on about getting her toenails cut, they catch on the sheet. I located Nurse Gillis and told her, only it must have slipped her mind because when I went across later on Mrs Maudsley was still on about it. I mentioned it again to Nurse Gillis just in case she'd forgotten and she said, 'I don't know how we managed before you came, Miss Schofield, I honestly don't.' Actually I found out later her toenails had been cut. Apparently Nurse Conkie must have cut them the same day as she cut mine, the day before yesterday, only Mrs Maudsley wouldn't know because she's no feeling in her feet.

Mrs Boothman's another of my regulars. Can't move. Can't speak. Doesn't bother me. I sit and chat away to her as if it was the most normal thing in the world. She'll sometimes manage a little movement of her hand, but the look in her eyes is enough.

Miss Brunskill's been down to see me. Nobody else much. Plenty of cards. I've got more cards than anybody else on this side.

She reads them.

'Feel kinda sick without you. Trish.' Trish Trotter. Picture of an elephant. 'Wishing you a speedy recovery. All in 406.' 'It's not the same without you. You're missed more than words can tell. So I'm sending this card to say, Please hurry and get well.' It says 'from all on the fifth floor' but I bet it's Mr Skidmore, it's such a classy card. A thatched cottage. I should imagine it can be damp, though, thatch. Silly one from Mr Cresswell and Mr Rudyard. 'Sorry you're sick. Hope you'll soon be back to normal. Whatever that is!'

I thought they might have been popping down, but Mr Cresswell hates hospitals, apparently, and they're going in for a new dog. A Dandy Dinmont. They think it'll be company for Tina, their Jack Russell. Well, they're out all day.

Pause.

Miss Brunskill's knitting me a bedjacket. I said, 'You'll have to be sharp, I shall be home next week.'

Pause.

I've got one nice neighbour, one not so nice. She's been quite ill. Just lies on her side all day. Karen, her name is. I offered her one of my women's books but she just closed her eyes. She's young. But however poorly I was I think I'd still try to be pleasant. The woman this side is as different again. Very outgoing. Talks the whole time. She's in with her chest. She's a lifelong smoker, so I don't wonder. Her daughter's marrying a computer programmer whose father was a prisoner of the Japanese, and she's inundated with visitors. She's a big TV fan so she's often down the other end. I reckon to be asleep sometimes when she's going on. You can't always be on your toes.

Pause.

Could just drink a cup of tea. Can't when you're having an op. They get you up at six, apparently. Give you a jab. Nurse Trickett says I won't even know I've gone and I'll be back up here by twelve. I've warned sister I shan't be able to get the papers, she thinks they'll manage.

Pause.

Solve the mystery anyway.

GO TO BLACK.

Still of the bedhead. Bed empty, as if she has gone for her operation.

GO TO BLACK AND UP AGAIN.

Miss Schofield is sitting by a radiator near a window in her dressing gown.

Hair in my dinner again today. Second time this week. Someone must be moulting. I mentioned it to Sister and she said she'd take it up with the kitchen staff and get back to me. She hasn't though. It isn't that she's nasty. Just crisp. I don't complain. Nurse Gillis can be sharp as well, but I try and meet her half-way. I said, 'Don't apologise. I deal with people myself. They don't realise, do they?'

Pause.

I'd such a shock yesterday. Nurse Conkie and Nurse Trickett had just given me my bath, and the little trainee nurse with the bonny face and cold hands was combing my hair, when I bethought me of the bedjacket Miss Brunskill had knitted me. I'd put it away in my locker because she'd made it too tight round the sleeves, but I tried it on again and it was just right. She says she hates knitting. I'm the only person she'll knit for, apparently. Of course, I paid for the wool. She's never ailed a thing, Miss Brunskill. Still, I hadn't until this do. Anyway I'd just got the bedjacket on and she'd fetched Nurse Conkie to see how nice I looked and they got me out my lipstick and I put a bit of that on. I was just sitting there and Nurse Conkie said, 'All dressed up and nowhere to go,' and a voice said, 'Hello. Long time no see!' And it's Mr Skidmore!

And I said it, loud, like that 'Mr Skidmore!' I said to him, I said, 'Five minutes earlier and you'd have seen me being bathed.' He said 'That's the story of my life.' We laughed.

He chatted about work. Said they were still only limping along. Said my job is open whenever I feel up to it and what's more it'll stay that way. They've got a special dispensation from Mr Strudwick. He says it's open-ended. They've never done that before. When Wendy Walsh had her infected sinus they ended up giving her a deadline. Still she wasn't the lynch-pin I am.

He did say there were other factors quite unconnected pushing them towards some degree of revamping. 'But,' he said, and patted my hand, 'in that event we shall find you a niche.' I said, 'Well I'm honoured. Fancy making a special journey for me.' Only it transpires that Mrs Skidmore's mother is in the psychiatric wing with another of her depression do's, and he'd left Mrs Skidmore sitting with her while he popped along to see me. 'Killing two birds with one stone,' he said. Then realised. 'I didn't mean that,' he said. 'Don't be silly,' I said. We laughed. He does look young when he laughs.

He'd just gone when Nurse Conkie came down to turn Mrs Boothman over. Great big smile. 'Who was your gentleman friend?' she said. She's got a nice sense of humour. I said 'That was my boss. He says they can't wait till I'm back.' 'I'm not sure we can spare you,' she said. We laughed.

I've been here the longest now, apart from Mrs Boothman and she's been resuscitated once. I potter around doing this and that.

Mr Penry-Jones is very proud of my scar. He fetches his

students round to see it nearly every week. He says he's never seen a scar heal as quickly as mine. It's to do with the right mental attitude apparently. They stop longer at my bed than with anybody. What he does is take the students a bit away, talks to them quietly, then they come up, one by one and ask me questions. I whisper to them 'He doesn't know what it is, so don't worry if you don't.' Mrs Durrant on this side, she won't have them. She goes on about 'patients' rights'. She's a school-teacher, though you'd never guess it to look at her. Long hair, masses of it. And I've heard her swear when they've given her a jab.

Pause.

I have a laugh with the porters that take me down for treatment. There's one in particular, Gerald. He's always pleased when it turns out to be me. 'My sweetheart,' he calls me. 'It's my sweetheart.' He's black too. I get on with everybody.

Pause.

I've started coming and looking out of this window. I just find it's far enough. There's naught much to see. There's the place where they put the bins out and a cook comes out now and again and has a smoke. And there's just the corner of the nurses' annexe. A young lad comes there with a nurse. He kisses her then goes away. Always the same lad. Nice. Though I don't like a lot of kissing, generally.

Pause.

I keep wondering about my Dad.

GO TO BLACK.

Up on a jug and tumbler on the bedside table.

BLACK.

Up again on Miss Schofield in bed. Her hair should be straight, as if it has been washed but not set. The speeches are more disjointed, and feebler.

I'm lucky. I'm standard size. I've got stuff off the peg and people have thought I'd had it run up specially. I've got a little fawn coat hanging up at home that I got fifteen years ago at Richard Shops. I ring the changes with scarves and gloves and whatnot, but it's been a grand little coat.

Pause.

I fetched up ever such a lot of phlegm this morning. Nurse Gillis was on. She was pleased. She said I'd fetched up more phlegm than anyone else on the ward. I said 'Was there a prize?' She laughed. I've never had that trouble before, but that's the bugbear when you're lying in bed, congestion.

Pause.

She said it's a good job all the patients aren't as little trouble as me or else half the nurses would be out of work. Funny, I didn't use to like her, but she's got a lot nicer lately. Her boy friend's a trainee something-or-other. I forget what. She did tell me. They're planning on moving to Australia.

Pause.

I've never been to Australia. She said if I wanted I could come out and visit them. I said, 'Yes.' Only I couldn't go. I couldn't be doing with all that sun.

Pause.

When Princess Alexandra came round this was the bed she stopped at, apparently.

Pause.

Sister's been better lately, too. The one I can't stand is Nurse Conkie. Never stops smiling. Great big smile. When they took old Mrs Boothman away just the same. Great big smile.

Pause.

Vicar round today. Think it was today. Beard. Sports jacket. Student, I thought, at first.

Pause.

Chatted. Bit before he got round to God. Says God singles you out for suffering. If you suffer shows you're somebody special in the eyes of God. He said he knew this from personal experience. His wife suffers from migraine.

Pause.

Do without being somebody special, this lot.

Pause.

There's a vicar goes round at Farnley, where my Dad is. Sits.

Pause.

Miss Brunskill came. Revolution at work. 406 and 405 knocked into one. Do your own photocopying now. Do it yourself, cut out the middleman. I said, 'Where did I fit in?' and she was telling me, only I must have dropped off and when I woke up she'd gone. Niche somewhere.

Pause.

I've been lucky with buses when I think back. I don't know what it is but just as I get to the bus stop up comes the bus. It must be a knack. I don't think I've ever had to wait more than two minutes for a bus, even when it's been a really spasmodic service.

Pause.

I wish they wouldn't laugh.

Pause.

There shouldn't be laughing.

Pause.

If they just left me alone I should be all right. 'Schofield, Margaret, Miss.' I've got a fly: keeps coming down. Must like me. There's a woman comes over and talks to me sometimes. Telling some tale. I close my eyes.

Pause.

Somebody was telling me about Rhyl. Still very select, apparently. No crowds.

Pause.

Here's my friend. This fly.

She smiles.

I said to Nurse Gillis, 'It's singled me out.' She laughed.

GO TO BLACK THEN UP. *The final shot is of an empty bed with the mattress folded back. The light is hard and white.*

FADE OUT.

INTRODUCTION TO
TALKING HEADS

These six monologues were written and recorded for BBC television in 1987. Forms, one is often led to think, dictate themselves, the material demanding to be written in a particular way and no other. I would be happy to think this were so with these pieces but I'm not sure it's true. *A Chip in the Sugar*, for instance, or *Bed Among the Lentils* could both have been written as plays proper. It would be fun to see Mr Turnbull, Mrs Whittaker's fancy man, in the flesh (and his three-quarter-length windcheater), or Mrs Shrubsole doing her ruthless flower arranging – see them for ourselves, that is, rather than through the eyes of Graham and Susan who narrate those respective stories. But then they would be different stories, more objective, rounded and altogether fairer to the people the narrator is talking about. None of these narrators after all is telling the whole story. Geoffrey, Susan's husband, may be a nicer, more forbearing man than her account of him might lead us to suppose; and Mr Turnbull may not be quite the common fellow ('could have been a bookie') the jealous Graham is so ready to disparage. And were these monologues plays there would be room for qualification and extenuation, allowances could be made, redemptions hinted at, a different point of view. Instead there is a single point of view, that of the speaker alone with the camera, and with the rest of the story pictured and peopled by the viewer more effort is demanded of the imagination. In this sense to watch a monologue on the screen is closer to reading a short story than watching a play.

Admittedly it is a stripped-down version of a short story, the style of its telling necessarily austere. 'Said' or 'says' is generally all that is required to introduce reported speech, because whereas the novelist or short story writer has a battery of expressions to choose from ('exclaimed', 'retorted', 'groaned', 'lisped'), in live narration such terms seem literary and self-conscious. Adverbs too ('she remarked, tersely') seem to over-egg the pudding or else acquire undue weight in the mouth of a supposedly artless narrator. And these narrators are artless. They don't quite know what they are saying and are telling a story to the meaning of which they are not entirely privy. In *A Chip in the Sugar* Graham would not accept that he is married to his mother, or Miss Ruddock in *A Lady of Letters* that she is not a public-spirited guardian of morals. In *Soldiering On* Muriel ends up knowing her husband ruined her daughter but is no closer to realising that she had a hand in it too. Lesley in *Her Big Chance* thinks she has a great deal to offer both as an actress and a person, and Susan, the vicar's wife in *Bed Among the Lentils*, doesn't realise it's not just the woman in the off-licence but the whole parish that knows she's on the drink. Only Doris, the old lady who has fallen and broken her hip in *A Cream Cracker Under the Settee*, knows the score and that she is done for, but though she can see it's her determination to dust that's brought about her downfall, what she doesn't see is that it's the same obsession that tidied her husband into the grave.

I am disturbed as I was with a previous collection of television plays to note so many repetitions and recurrences. There are droves of voluntary workers, umpteen officials from the social services, and should there be a knock on the door it's most likely to be a bearded vicar. Even Emily Brontë turns up twice. If I'm guilty of repeating myself, on another count I plead innocence. The suspicion of child abuse in *A Lady of Letters* and the hint of it in *Soldiering On* might suggest I am straining after topicality. My instinct is generally to take flight in the opposite direction and in fact both these pieces were written and recorded before the subject began regularly to hit the headlines, which it may well have ceased to do by the time the programmes are transmitted. Since several of the characters fare badly at the hands of social and community workers I might seem to be taking a currently fashionable line here also. In the popular press nowadays social workers are generally (and easily) abused. I have little experience of them and to seem to line up with the *Sun* or the *Daily Express* would dismay me. My quarrel with social work is not with its praiseworthy practicalities but with the jargon in which it's sometimes conducted. Graham's 'I am not being defensive about sexual intercourse; she is my mother' is a protest about language.

Some of the events in these stories stem from actual occurrences in my life, though they are often joined to it by a very narrow isthmus. The funeral with which *Soldiering On* begins (though none of the characters in it) was suggested by the funeral of the composer George Fenton's father, who had been in Colditz and like Ralph had touched life at many points. Though much of the church stuff in *Bed Among the Lentils* (including Mr Medlicott the verger) comes from my childhood, the disaffection of Susan, the vicar's wife, I can trace to opening a hymn book in the chapel of Giggleswick School and finding in tiny, timid letters on the fly leaf, 'Get lost, Jesus'. Of these six characters only Lesley, the small-part actress, is wholly modern (while being quite old-fashioned). She and dozens like her have auditioned for films and plays I've done in the last twenty years. One of the first Lesley-like characters was a boy who came up for a part in *Forty Years On*. The director asked him what he had done:

> 'I was in George Bernard Shaw.'
> 'What did you play?'
> 'The drums.'

Perky, undefeated, their hopes of stardom long since gone, these actors retail the films and plays one might have glimpsed them in, playing waiters or barmen or, like Lesley, travelling on the back of a farm cart next to the star, wearing a shawl, the shawl 'original nineteenth-century embroidery, all hand done'. I saw an actor for a part not long ago who had been in a few episodes of *Emmerdale Farm*. 'I played the postman,' he said, 'only I haven't done any since. They don't seem to be getting much mail.'

Another obsession goes back to childhood. The dog dirt outside Buckingham Palace that spoils Miss Ruddock's Away-day and the 'little hairs all up and down' that rule out a dog for Doris betray a prejudice inherited from my father, who was a butcher in Leeds. He was plagued by dogs: 'Get out, you nasty lamppost-smelling little article,' he shouted once as he raced some unfortunate mongrel from the shop, and now thirty years later Doris has the line. It was my father too who had a craze for fretwork, but whereas for Doris's husband Wilfred fretwork is just one of his dreams ('toys and forts and whatnot, no end of money he was going to make'), with Dad it was no dream.

Sitting at his little treadle saw with plans from *Hobbies Magazine* beside him he made forts and farms for my brother and me, a toy butcher's shop once and wonderfully elaborate constructions of ramps and trapdoors into which we shot marbles. This was at the start of the Second War when toys were scarce, and for a few years he was able to make a little money selling some of his stuff to a toyshop down County Arcade off Briggate. It wasn't much though. 'You want to ask a bit more,' my mam used to say. 'They take advantage of you. That's your trouble, Walt, you won't push yourself.' Which sounds like Doris again. Toy penguins were Dad's speciality, made out of three-ply and set on a sturdy green four-wheeled cart. Did we ever come across a child pulling one of these creations it was a big event and we would trail behind, scanning the face of its small owner for any evidence of pleasure in this (to me very dull) toy, Dad presumably experiencing some of the same pleasure a writer gets when he catches someone reading his book.

It's with mixed feelings that I see tattoos are (twice) sniffed at, along with red paint, yellow gloves and two-tone cardigans. These disparagements too date back to home and childhood, where they were items in a catalogue of disapproval that ranged through (fake) leopardskin coats, dyed (blonde) hair to slacks, cocktail cabinets and statuettes of ladies with alsatian dogs on leash. In our house and in my mother's idiosyncratic scheme of things they were all common. Common is not an easy term to define without seeming to brand the user as snobbish or socially pretentious, which my mother wasn't. But it was always her distinction: I never remember my father making it, and both in its use and application common tended to be a woman's term. 'She's a common woman' one heard more often (was more common) than 'He's a common feller', perhaps because in those days women had more time and inclination to make such distinctions. A common woman was likely to swear or drink (or drink 'shorts'), to get all dolled up and go out leaving the house upside down and make no bones about having affairs. Enjoy herself, possibly, and that was the trouble; a common woman sidestepped her share of the proper suffering of her sex. What was also being criticised was an element of pretension and display (the dyed blonde hair, the too-tight slip-over, the face plastered with make-up). Elsie Tanner was a common woman, as with her curlers and too ready opinions is Hilda Ogden. And so, I thought as a child, was Mary Magdalene.

Sudden money augmented the risk and pools winners would find it hard to avoid the epithet. Hence the unfortunate tale of Vivien Nicholson, the Yorkshire pools winner and heroine of Jack Rosenthal's *Spend, Spend, Spend*. Her persistent car crashes and the dramas and notorieties of her personal life were never out of the *Evening Post*. 'Well,' my mother used to say, as Mrs N wrote off yet another of her cars and her lovers in some frightful motorway pile-up, 'she's a common woman.' No other explanation was necessary.

Places could be common too, particularly at the seaside. Blackpool was common (people enjoying themselves), Morecambe less so (not enjoying themselves as much), and Grange or Lytham not common at all (enjoyment not really on the agenda). If we ever did get to Blackpool we stayed at Cleveleys or Bispham, the refined end. To my brother and me (and I suspect to the local estate agents) refined just meant furthest away from the funfair. Not that where we stayed made much difference to the type of boarding house or the mixed bag we found there. To some extent my mother's nice distinctions were subjective and self-fulfilling: we met a better class of person where we stayed because we kept out of the way of the rest, Palm Court rather than bathing beauties, not the knobbly knees contest but a Wallace Arnold to Windermere. Package holidays came too late for my parents but had they ever ventured abroad they would have taken their attitudes with them. My mam would soon have located the Bispham end of Benidorm, a select part to Sitges. 'Well, we don't like it all hectic, do we, Dad?'

Common persists. It's not a distinction I'd want to be detected making but to myself I make it still. There are some lace (or more likely nylon) curtains popular nowadays that are gathered up for some reason in the middle. They look to me like a woman who's been to the lav and got her underskirt caught up behind her. They're absurd but that's not my real objection. They're common. The mock Georgian doorways that disfigure otherwise decent houses, the so-called Kentucky fried Georgian, offend me because they're cheap, inappropriate, ill-proportioned... and common.

Finally vicars who, Anglican though not always specified as such, turn up in all but one of these pieces, earnest, visitant and resolutely contemporary. Several are bearded, one is in trainers and most are in mufti. I have no particular wish to lock the clergy out of the wardrobe or ban them the boutique, but along with postmen and porters I wish they had not abandoned black. Just as postmen nowadays look like members of the Rumanian airforce so cassocks come in beige and even lilac, and if a parson submits to the indignity of a dog collar the chances are it has gone slimline, peeping coyly above a modish number in some fetching pastel shade. Nuns too have lost their old billowing, wimpled innocence and now look like prison wardresses on the loose. Even hearses have gone grey, black altogether too uncompromising a colour, life something to be shaded out of when, after much suffering tastefully borne, we blend nicely into the grave.

The clergy not wanting to look the part has something to do with the dismantling of the Book of Common Prayer. Anxious not to sound like parsons they can hardly be blamed for not wanting to look like them either. The 'underneath this cassock I am but a man like any other' act that Geoff does in *Bed Among the Lentils* must be a familiar routine at many a church door. And it's not of course new. Priests have always hankered after the world, or at any rate the worldly, and consorting as He did with publicans and sinners it was Jesus who started the rot. Or so Susan would say.

I don't know why it should be only Catholics who are thought never to escape their religious upbringing; I have never managed to outgrow mine. When I was sixteen and not long confirmed I was devoutly religious, a regular communicant who knew the service off by heart. It might be thought this would rejoice a vicar's heart and maybe it did, but actually I think the parish clergy found my fervour faintly embarrassing. A fervent Anglican is a bit of a contradiction in terms anyway, but I was conscious that my constant presence at the Eucharist, often midweek as well as Sundays, was thought to be rather unhealthy. As the celebrant sallied forth from the vestry on a cold winter's morning and found me sitting or (like Miss Frobisher, never one to let an opportunity slip) getting in a spot of silent prayer, he must have felt like a doctor opening the surgery door and discovering the sole occupant of the waiting room some tiresome hypochondriac (I was that too actually). Shy, bespectacled and innocent of the world I knew I was a disappointment to the clergy. What they wanted were brands to pluck from the burning and that was not me by a long chalk; I'd never even been near the fire.

Those early morning services with just a handful of regulars in the side chapel, the others generally maiden ladies who had cycled there on tall bicycles through the autumn mists, were to me the stuff of religion, the real taste of God. But though I did not admit it myself I knew that what the clergy preferred were occasions like Christmas Eve when the church was packed to the doors, the side aisles full, people even standing at the back like they did in those days at the cinema. For many in the congregation this was their one visit to church in the year. Plumping to my knees with split-second timing I would scornfully note how few of these festive communicants knew the service. Most of them didn't even kneel but sat, head in hand as if they were on the lavatory, this their one spiritual evacuation of the year.

Fastidious worshipper that I was, when I got to the altar rail I was even more choosy. Christmas and Easter, those joyous festivals of the Christian year, figured in my calendar as fearful health hazards and a true test of faith. At the sparsely attended eucharists that were the norm the rest of the year one could bank on finding oneself at the communion rail alongside a person of proven piety and blameless life. As my turn came for the chalice I would think of the TB or the cancer I might catch but come the Watch Night services at Christmas and Easter these ailments were forgotten. Then it was VD that was the bugbear. With the church chock-a-block with publicans and sinners one never knew who was going to be one's drinking companion. It was all my mother's fault. She had brought us up never to share a lemonade bottle with other boys, and wiping it with your hand, she said, was no protection, so I knew the dainty dab with the napkin the priest gave the chalice made no difference at all. There was God of course, in whose omnipotence I was supposed to believe: He might run to some mystical antisepsis. But then He might not. That I should catch syphilis from the chalice might be all part of His plan. The other place I was frightened of contracting it was the seat of a public lavatory, and that the rim of the toilet should be thus linked with the rim of the chalice was also part of the wonderful mystery of God. It was on such questions of hygiene rather than any of theology that my faith cut its teeth. I see myself walking back from the altar and plunging to my knees, then at the first opportunity surreptitiously spitting into my handkerchief. But I knew that if God had marked me down for VD and a test of faith no amount of spitting was going to help. It was all chickenfeed to the Ancient of Days.

Switching on the Test Match at Headingley by mistake nowadays, I see the scene of these early spiritual struggles. 'Why, Headingley!' I might say, parodying Larkin, 'I was reborn here.' The camera pans along the Cardigan Road boundary and there above the trees is the spire of St Michael's, designed by J.L. Pearson who built Truro Cathedral, St Michael's with St Bartholomew's at Armley, the best of the nineteenth-century churches in Leeds, and in those days I knew them all. Around the time I was spitting into my handkerchief David Storey, the novelist and playwright, was playing rugby for Wakefield and so was often on the Headingley ground. For him too St Michael's was a symbol of hope. Cold, wet and frightened in the middle of a game he would look longingly at the spire and tell himself that within the hour he would be stood opposite the church waiting for a tram; the match would be over and he would be going home. That is by the way, but then so is much of this reminiscence, my childhood itself fairly by the way, or so it seemed at the time. Brought up in the provinces in the forties and fifties one learned early the valuable lesson that life is generally something that happens elsewhere.

A CHIP IN THE SUGAR

Graham · Alan Bennett

GRAHAM IS A MILD MIDDLE-AGED MAN. THE PLAY IS SET IN HIS BEDROOM, A SMALL ROOM WITH ONE WINDOW AND ONE DOOR. IT IS FURNISHED WITH A SINGLE BED, A WARDROBE, TWO CHAIRS AND NOTHING MUCH ELSE.

I'd just taken her tea up this morning when she said, 'Graham, I think the world of you.' I said, 'I think the world of you.' And she said, 'That's all right then.' I said, 'What's brought this on?' She said, 'Nothing. This tea looks strong, pull the curtains.' Of course I knew what had brought it on. She said, 'I wouldn't like you to think you're not Number One.' So I said, 'Well, you're Number One with me too. Give me your teeth. I'll swill them.'

What it was we'd had a spot of excitement yesterday: we ran into a bit of Mother's past. I said to her, 'I didn't know you had a past. I thought I was your past.' She said, 'You?' I said, 'Well, we go back a long way. How does he fit in vis-à-vis Dad?' She laughed. 'Oh, he was pre-Dad.' I said, 'Pre-Dad? I'm surprised you remember him, you don't remember to switch your blanket off.' She said, 'That's different. His name's Turnbull.' I said, 'I know. He said.'

I'd parked her by the war memorial on her usual seat while I went and got some reading matter. Then I waited while she went and spent a penny in the disabled toilet. She's not actually disabled, her memory's bad, but she says she prefers their toilets because you get more elbow room. She always takes for ever, diddling her hands and whatnot, and when she eventually comes back it turns out she's been chatting to the attendant. I said, 'What about?' She said, 'Hanging. She was in favour of stiffer penalties for minor offences and I thought, "Well, we know better, our Graham and me." I wish you'd been there, love; you could have given her the statistics, where are we going for our tea?'

The thing about Mam is that though she's never had a proper education, she's picked up enough from me to be able to hold her own in discussions about up-to-the-minute issues like the environment and the colour problem, and for a woman of her age and background she has a very liberal slant. She'll look at my *Guardian* and she actually thinks for herself. Doctor Chaudhury said to me, 'Full marks, Graham. The best way to avoid a broken hip is to have a flexible mind. Keep up the good work.'

They go mad round the war memorial so when we cross over I'll generally slip my arm through hers until we're safely across, only once we're on the pavement she'll postpone letting it go, because once upon a time we got stopped by one of these questionnaire women who reckons to take us for husband and wife. I mean, Mam's got white hair. She was doing this dodge and I said, 'Mam, let go of my arm.' I didn't really wrench it, only next thing I knew she's flat on the pavement. I said, 'Oh my God, Mother.'

People gather round and I pick up her bag, and she sits up and says, 'I've laddered both my stockings.' I said, 'Never mind your stockings, what about your pelvis?' She says, 'It's these bifocals. They tell you not to look down. I was avoiding some sick.' Somebody says, 'That's a familiar voice,' and there's a little fellow bending over her, green trilby hat, shorty raincoat. 'Hello,' he says, 'remember me?'

Well, she doesn't remember people, I know for a fact because she swore me down she'd never met Joy Buckle, who teaches Flowers in Felt and Fabric at my day centre. I said, 'You have met Joy, you knitted her a tea cosy.' That's all she can knit, tea cosies. And bed socks. Both outmoded articles. I said to her, 'Branch out. If you can knit tea cosies you can knit skiing hats.' She says, 'Well, I will.' Only I have to stand over her or else she'll still leave a hole for the spout. 'Anyway,' I said, 'you do remember Joy because you said she had some shocking eyebrows.' She said, 'I hope you didn't tell her that.' I said, 'Of course I didn't.' She said, 'Well, I don't remember.' And that's the way she is, she doesn't remember and here's this little fellow saying, 'Do you remember me?' So I said, 'No she won't. Come on, Mother. Let's get you up.' Only she says, 'Remember you? Of course. It's Frank Turnbull. It must be fifty years.' He said, 'Fifty-two. Filey. 1934.' She said, 'Sea-Crest.' He said, 'No sand in the bedrooms.' And they both cracked out laughing.

Meanwhile she's still stuck on the cold pavement. I said, 'Come along, Mother. We don't want piles.' Only he butts in again. He says, 'With respect, it's advisable not to move a person until it's been ascertained no bones are broken. I was in the St John's Ambulance Brigade.' 'Yes,' said Mother, 'and who did you learn your bandaging on?' And they both burst out laughing again. He had on these bright yellow gloves, could have been a bookie.

Eventually, I get my arms round her waist and hoist her up, only his lordship's no help as he claims to have a bad back. When I've finally got her restored to the perpendicular she introduces him. 'This is Frank Turnbull, a friend of mine from the old days.' What old days? First time I knew there were any old days. Turns out he's a gents' outfitter, semi-retired, shop in Bradford and some sort of outlet in Morecambe. I thought, 'Well, that accounts for the yellow gloves.'

Straight off he takes charge. He says, 'What you need now, Vera, is a cup of coffee.' I said, 'Well, we were just going for some tea, weren't we, Mother?' Vera! Her name's not Vera. She's never been called Vera. My Dad never called her Vera, except just once, when they were wheeling him into the theatre. Vera. 'Right,' he says, 'follow me.' And puts his arm through hers. 'Careful,' she says. 'You'll make my boy friend jealous.' I didn't say anything.

Pause.

Now the café we generally patronise is just that bit different. It's plain but it's classy, no cloths on the tables, the menu comes on a little slate and the waitresses wear their own clothes and look as if they're doing it just for the fun of it. The stuff's all home-made and we're both big fans of the date and walnut bread. I said, 'This is the place.' Mr Turnbull goes straight past. 'No,' he says, 'I know somewhere, just opened. Press on.'

Now, if there's one thing Mother and me are agreed on it's that red is a common colour. And the whole place is done out in red. Lampshades red. Waitresses in red. Plates red, and on the tables those plastic sauce things got up to look like tomatoes. Also red. And when I look there's a chip in the sugar. I thought, 'Mother won't like this.' 'Oh,' she says, 'this looks cheerful, doesn't it, Graham?' I said, 'There's a chip in the sugar.' 'A detail,' he says, 'they're still having their teething troubles. Is it three coffees?' I said, 'We like tea,' only Mother says, 'No. I feel like an adventure. I'll have coffee.' He gets hold of the menu and puts his hand on hers. 'Might I suggest,' he says, 'a cheeseburger?' She said, 'Oh, what's that?' He said, 'It's fresh country beef, mingled with golden-fried onions, topped off with toasted cheese served with french fries and lemon wedge.' 'Oh, lemon wedge,' said Mother. 'That sounds nice.'

I thought, 'Well, I hope you can keep it down.' Because it'll be the pizza story all over again. One mouthful and at four o'clock in the morning I was still stuck at her bedside with the bucket. She said, 'I like new experiences in eating. I had a pizza once, didn't I, Graham?' I didn't say anything.

They fetch the food and she's wiring in. He said, 'Are you enjoying your cheeseburger?' She said, 'I am. Would I be mistaken in thinking that's tomato sauce?' He said, 'It is.' She says, 'Give us a squirt.' They both burst out laughing. He said, 'Glass cups, Graham. Be careful or we'll see up your nose.' More laughter. She said, 'Graham's quite refined. He often has a dry sherry.'

'Well, he could do with smartening up a bit,' Mr Turnbull said. 'Plastic mac. He wants one of these quilted jobs, I've shifted a lot of those.' 'I don't like those quilted jobs,' I said. 'He sweats,' Mother said. 'There's no excuse for that in this day and age,' Mr Turnbull said, 'the range of preparations there are on the market. You want to invest in some roll-on deodorant.' Everybody could hear. 'And flares are anathema even in Bradford.'

'Graham doesn't care, do you, Graham?' Mother said. 'He reads a lot.' 'So what?' Mr Turnbull said. 'I know several big readers who still manage to be men about town. Lovat green's a nice shade. I tell you this, Graham,' he said, 'if I were squiring a young lady like this around town I wouldn't do it in grey socks and sandals. These shoes are Italian. Feel.' 'I always think Graham would have made a good parson,' Mother said, feeling his foot, 'only he doesn't believe in God.' 'That's no handicap these days,' Mr Turnbull said. 'What do you do?'

'He's between jobs at present,' Mother said. 'He used to do soft toys for handicapped children. Then he was making paper flowers at one stage.' I went to the toilet.

Pause.

When I came back he said, 'I don't believe in mental illness. Nine times out of ten it's a case of pulling your socks up.' I didn't say anything. Mother said, 'Yes, well, I think the pendulum's gone too far.' She didn't look at me. 'It's like these girls, not eating,' he said, 'they'd eat if they'd been brought up like us, Vera, nothing to eat.' 'That's right,' Mother said, 'they have it too easy. Did you marry?' 'Twice,' he said. 'I buried Amy last May. I was heartbroken but life has to go on. I've a son lives in Stevenage. I've got two grandsons, one at the motorbike stage. Do you drive?' 'No,' I said. 'You do,' Mother said. 'You had that scooter.' 'It was only a moped,' I said. 'Well, a moped, Graham. They're all the same. I can't get him to blow his own trumpet.'

'I've got a Rover 2000,' Mr Turnbull said, 'handles like a dream. I think the solution to mental illness is hard physical work. Making raffia mats, I'd go mad.' 'Yes,' says Mother, 'only they do pottery as well. I've seen some nice ashtrays.' 'Featherbedding,' Mr Turnbull said. 'Do you like these Pakistanis?' 'Well in moderation,' Mother said. 'We have a nice newsagent. Graham thinks we're all the same.' I said, 'I thought you did.' She said, 'Well, I do when you explain it all to me, Graham, but then I forget the explanation and I'm back to square one.' 'There is no explanation,' Mr Turnbull said. 'They sell mangoes in our post office, what explanation is there for that?' 'I know,' Mother said, 'I smelled curry on my *Woman's Own*. You have to be educated to understand.' I didn't say anything.

He ran us home, promised to give her a tinkle next time he was in the neighbourhood. Said he was often round here tracking down two-tone cardigans. 'Your Mother's a grand woman,' he said. 'You want to cherish her.' 'He does, he does,' Mother said. 'You're my boy friend, aren't you, Graham?' She put her arm through mine.

GO TO BLACK.

Come up on Graham standing looking out of the window. It is late afternoon. He sits on the arm of the chair.

There must be a famine on somewhere because we were just letting our midday meal go down when the vicar calls with some envelopes. Breezes in, anorak and running shoes, and he says, 'I always look forward to coming to this house, Mrs Whittaker.' (He's got the idea she's deaf, which she's not; it's one of the few things she isn't.) He says, 'Do you know why? It's because you two remind me of Jesus and his mother.' Well, I've always thought Jesus was a bit off-hand with his mother, and on one occasion I remember he was quite snotty with her, but I didn't say anything. And of course Madam is over the moon. In her book if you can't get compared with the Queen Mother the Virgin Mary's the next best thing. She says, 'Are you married?' (She asks him every time, never remembers.) He said, 'No, Mrs Whittaker. I am married to God.' She says, 'Where does that leave you with the housework?' He said, 'Well, I don't do as well as your Graham. He's got this place like a palace.' She says, 'Well, I do my whack. I washed four pairs of stockings this morning.' She hadn't. She put them in the bowl then they slipped her mind, so the rest of the operation devolved on me.

He said, 'How are you today, Mrs Whittaker?' She says,

'Stiff down one side.' I said, 'She had a fall yesterday.' She says, 'I never did.' I said, 'You did, Mother. You had a fall, then you ran into Mr Turnbull.'

Pause.

She says, 'That's right. I did.' And she starts rooting in her bag for her lipstick. She says, 'That's one of them anoraky things, isn't it? They've gone out now, those. If you want to look like a man about town you want to get one of those continental quilts.' He said, 'Oh?' I said, 'She means those quilted jackets.' She said, 'He knows what I mean. Where did you get those shoes?' He said, 'They're training shoes.' She said, 'Training for what? Are you not fully qualified?' He said, 'If Jesus were alive today, Mrs Whittaker, I think you'd find these were the type of shoes he would be wearing.' 'Not if his mother had anything to do with it,' she said. 'She'd have him down Stead and Simpson's and get him into some good brogues. Somebody was telling me the Italians make good shoes.'

The vicar takes this as his cue to start on about people who have no shoes at all and via this to the famine in Ethiopia. I fork out 50p which he says will feed six families for a week and she says, 'Well, it would have bought me some Quality Street.' When he's at the door he says, 'I take my hat off to you, Graham, I've got a mother myself.' When I get back in she said, 'Vicar! He looked more like the paper boy. How can you look up to somebody in pumps?' Just then there's a knock at the door. 'Get down,' she says, 'he's back.' Only it isn't. It's Mr Turnbull.

Graham stands up.

New outfit this time: little suede coat, corduroy collar, maroon trousers. She says, 'You're colourful.' 'We just happen to have these slacks on offer,' he says. 'I was wondering whether you fancied a run out to Bolton Abbey?' 'Bolton Abbey?' she says. 'Oh, that's right up our street, isn't it, Graham? Graham's good with buildings, aren't you, Graham? He knows all the periods of houses. There's one period that's just come in. Other people don't like it yet but we do, don't we, Graham?' 'I don't know,' I said. 'You do. What is it?' 'Victorian,' I said. 'That's it, Victorian. Only there's a lot been pulled down.' Mr Turnbull yawns. 'I've got a little bungalow.' 'That's nice,' Mother says. 'I like a nice bungalow, don't you, Graham?' 'Yes,' I said, 'provided it's not a blot on the landscape.' 'Mine's architect designed,' says Mr Turnbull. 'It has a patio and a breakfast bar, it overlooks a beauty spot.' 'Oh,' said Mother, 'sounds tip-top. We'd better be getting our skates on, Graham.' He said, 'I've got to pick up a load of green three-quarter-length wind-cheaters in Ilkley; there won't really be room for a third party. Isn't there anything on at the pictures?' 'Oh he'll be happy reading,' Mother said. 'Won't you, Graham?' 'Anyway,' Mr Turnbull said, 'you don't always want to be with your Mother at your age, do you, Graham?' I didn't say anything.

He sits on the chair arm again.

I've been laid on my bed reading one of my magazines. I've a feeling that somebody's looking at the house, only I can't see anybody. Once or twice I think I've heard a knock on the door, but I haven't gone in case there's nobody there.

GO TO BLACK.

Come up on Graham sitting on his unmade bed in his pyjamas. Night.

Today they went over to York. It was after seven when he dropped her off. He generally comes in but not this time. Just gives her a little kiss. She has to bend down. I said, 'Have you had a good time?' She said, 'Yes. We had egg and chips, tea, bread and butter, we've got a lot in common and there's a grand new car park.' I said, 'Did you go in the Minster?' She said, 'No. Frank's not keen on old buildings. We need to look more to the future. He says they've built a spanking new precinct in Bradford, so that's going to be next on the agenda. You're quiet.' I said, 'Well, do you wonder? Doctor Chaudhury says I should have a stable environment. This isn't a stable environment with your fancy men popping in every five minutes.' She said, 'He isn't my fancy man.' I said, 'Well, he's your fancy man in embryo.' She said, 'You know I don't know what that means.' I said, 'How old are you?' She said, 'I don't know.' I said, 'You do know.' She said, 'I don't. Tell me.' I said, 'You're seventy-two.' 'That's not so old. How old was Winston Churchill?' I said, 'When?' She said, 'You think you've got it over me, Graham Whittaker. Well, I'll tell you something, my memory's better with Frank. He was telling me about the economy. You've got it all wrong.' I said, 'How?' 'I can't remember but you have. Blaming it on the government. Frank says it's the blacks.' I didn't say anything, just came upstairs.

When I went down again she's still sat there with her hat and coat on. I said: 'Do you want to knit him a tea cosy?' She said, 'I don't think he's the tea-cosy type. When I first knew him he had a motorbike and sidecar. Besides, I think it's got beyond the tea-cosy stage.' I said, 'What do you mean?' She said, 'Graham.

My one aim in life is for you to be happy. If I thought that by dying I would make you happy I would.' I said, 'Mother, your dying wouldn't make me happy. In fact the reverse. It would make me unhappy. Anyway, Mother, you're not going to die.' She said, 'No. I'm not going to die. I'm going to get married. And the honeymoon is in Tenerife. Have one of your tablets.'

She made a cup of tea. I said, 'How can you go to Tenerife, you're smothered at Scarborough?' She said, 'It's a four-star hotel with tip-top air-conditioning, you get your breakfast from a long table.' I said, 'What about your bowels?' She said, 'What about my bowels?' 'Well, you said they were unpredictable at Morecambe. Get them to the Canary Islands and they're going to be all over the place.' She said, 'Who's talking about the Canary Islands? I'm going to Tenerife.' 'And what about post-Tenerife? Where are you going to live?' She said, 'Here. Frank says he'll be away on and off on business but he wants to call this home.' I said, 'What about me?' She went into the kitchen. 'Well, we wondered whether you'd prefer to go back to the hostel. You were happy at the hostel. You rubbed shoulders with all sorts.' I said, 'Mam. This is my home.' She said, 'A man shouldn't be living with his mother at your age, Frank says. Did you take a tablet?'

Now it's four o'clock in the morning and I can't sleep. There's a car parked outside. I can't see but I think there's somebody in it, watching like they used to do before. I thought all that chapter was closed.

GO TO BLACK.

Come up on Graham sitting on an upright chair. Evening.

This morning I went to Community Caring down at the Health Centre. It caters for all sorts. Steve, who runs it, is dead against what he calls 'the ghetto approach'. What he's after is a nice mix of personality difficulties as being the most fruitful exercise in problem-solving and a more realistic model of society generally. There's a constant flow of coffee, 'oiling the wheels' Steve calls it, and we're all encouraged to ventilate our problems and generally let our hair down. I sometimes feel a bit out of it as I've never had any particular problems, so this time when Steve says 'Now chaps and chappesses who's going to set the ball rolling?' I get in quick and tell them about Mother and Mr Turnbull. When I'd finished Steve said, 'Thank you, Graham, for sharing your problem with us. Does anybody want to kick it around?'

First off the mark is Leonard, who wonders whether Graham has sufficiently appreciated that old people can fall in love and have meaningful relationships generally, the same as young people. I suppose this is understandable coming from Leonard because he's sixty-five, only he doesn't have meaningful relationships. He's been had up for exposing himself in Sainsbury's doorway. As Mother said, 'Tesco, you could understand it.'

Then Janice chips in. 'Had they been having sexual intercourse?' I said I didn't want to think about it. Steve said, 'Why?' I said I didn't know. So he said, 'Maybe what we should be talking about is why Graham is being so defensive about sexual intercourse.' I said, 'Steve. I am not being defensive about sexual intercourse. She is my mother.' Jackie, who's nine parts Lesbian, said, 'Graham. She is also A Woman.' I couldn't believe this. I said, 'Jackie. You're an ex-battered wife. I thought you didn't approve of marriage.' She said, 'Graham. I approve of caring marriage.' I said, 'Jackie. This is not caring marriage.' She said, 'Graham, what's Tenerife? That's caring. All I got was a black eye and a day trip to Fleetwood.' Then they all have a go. Get Graham. Steve summed up. 'The general feeling of the group is that Graham could be more open.' I said, 'How can I be more open? There's somebody sat outside the house watching.' I wanted to discuss that only Leonard leaped in and said he felt the need to talk through an episode behind British Home Stores. I stuck it a bit longer and then came home.

Mother's sat there, all dolled up. Earrings on, chiffon scarf, lathered in make-up. She said, 'Oh, I thought you were Mr Turnbull.' I said, 'No.' She said, 'I'll just go to the lav.' She goes three times in the next ten minutes. I said, 'You're not getting married today, are you?' She said, 'No. There's a new Asda superstore opened at Bingley and we thought we'd give it the once over. Frank says they have a very good selection of sun tan lotions.' I said, 'Mother, there's somebody watching the house.' She said, 'I want to pick out some tissues and Frank's looking for a little chammy for his windscreen. He's promised me something called a cheeseburger, there's a café that's part of the complex.'

Just then there's a little toot on the horn and she runs to the lav again. I said, 'Don't go. Don't leave me, Mam.' She said, 'I'm not giving in to you, you're a grown man. Is my underskirt showing?' He toots again. She says, 'Look at your magazines, make yourself a poached egg.' I said, 'Mam.' She said, 'There's that bit of chicken in the fridge. You could iron those two vests. Take a tablet. Give us a kiss. Toodle pip.'

I thought I'd go sit in the back room where they couldn't see me. I pulled the curtains and I'm sitting there in the dark and I think I hear a knock at the front door. I don't move and there's another knock. Louder. I do like Doctor Chaudhury says and tell myself it's not happening, only it is. Somebody shouts through the letter-box. 'I know you're in there. Open this door.' So I do. And there is someone. It's a woman.

She said, 'Are you the son?' I said, 'What?' She said, 'Are you the son? I'm the daughter.' I said, 'Have you been watching the house?' She said, 'On and off. Why?' I said, 'Nothing.' She said, 'I don't know what there is to look so suited about.' I said, 'You'd better come in.'

GO TO BLACK.

Come up on Graham as he puts a magazine on top of the wardrobe. He sits down in the easy chair. Night.

It's nine o'clock when I hear the car outside. I'm sitting watching TV. I say, 'Oh hello. Did you have a nice time?' She said, 'Yes. Yes we did, thank you.' 'Did you get your sun tan lotion?' She said, 'What sun tan lotion?' 'You were going to get some sun tan lotion. Never mind. You've forgotten. How's Mr Turnbull?' 'Frank? He's all right.' She took her things off. 'I'm sure you could get to like him, Graham, if only you got to know him.' I said, 'Well, you should have brought him in.' 'Well, I will next time. It'd be nice if now and again we could go off as a threesome. What have you done?' 'Nothing,' I said. 'Just sat here.' 'You've been all right?' 'Mmm.'

'You see,' she said, 'there wasn't anybody outside.' 'Oh yes there was.' She said, 'Oh Graham. Have you had a tablet? Have a tablet.' 'I don't want a tablet. I'll tell you who was sat outside. Mrs Pamela Musgrave.' She said, 'Who's she?' 'Née Turnbull. The daughter of your hubby to be.' She said, 'He hasn't got a daughter. He's got a son down south. He hasn't got a daughter,' she said, 'you're making stuff up now, have a tablet.' I said, 'I'm not making it up. And there's something else I'm not making up. Mrs Turnbull.' She said, 'There isn't a Mrs Turnbull. She's dead. I'm going to the lav.' I said, 'She's not dead. She's in a wheelchair with a broken heart. He's been having you on.'

After a bit she comes out. 'You're just saying all this.' 'The number's on the pad. Ring up. She's disabled is his wife. Has been for ten years. Their daughter looks after them. You're not the first. He's always doing it. One woman, it was going to be Barbados. Somebody spotted you together at Bolton Abbey. A well-wisher. Tenerife!'

Later on I took her a cup of tea. She'd been crying. She said, 'I bought this little bedjacket.' I said, 'I'm sorry, Mam.' She said, 'He was right enough. What can you expect at my age? How old am I?' 'Seventy-two.' 'That's another thing. I remembered with him. I don't remember with you.' I said, 'I'm sorry.' She said, 'You're not sorry. How are you sorry? You didn't like him.' I said, 'He wasn't good enough for you.' She said, 'I'm the best judge of that. He was natty, more than can be said for you.' And starts crying again. I said, 'I understand, Mam.' She said, 'You don't understand. How can you understand, you, you're not normal?' I said, 'I'm going to bed.'

In a bit she comes shouting outside the door. 'You think you've got it over me, Graham Whittaker. Well, you haven't. I've got it over you.' I said, 'Go back to bed.' She said, 'I know the kind of magazines you read.' I said, 'Chess. You'll catch cold.' She said, 'They never are chess. Chess with no clothes on. Chess in their birthday suits. That kind of chess. Chess men.' I said, 'Go to bed. And turn your blanket off.'

Pause.

Next day she's right as rain. Forgotten it. Never mentions it anyway, except just as we're coming out of the house she said, 'I do love you, Graham.' I said, 'I love you too.' She said, 'Anyway he had a hearing aid.' She said, 'What's on the agenda for today, then?' I said, 'I thought we might have a little ride to Ripon.' She said, 'Oh yes, Ripon. That's nice. We could go to the cathedral. We like old buildings, don't we, you and me?'

She put her arm through mine.

FADE OUT.

BED AMONG THE LENTILS

Susan · Maggie Smith

SUSAN IS A VICAR'S WIFE. SHE IS THIN AND NERVOUS AND PROBABLY SMOKES. SHE SITS ON AN UPRIGHT CHAIR IN THE KITCHEN. IT IS EVENING.

Geoffrey's bad enough but I'm glad I wasn't married to Jesus. The lesson this morning was the business in the Garden of Gethsemane when Jesus prays and the disciples keep falling asleep. He wakes them up and says, 'Could you not watch with me one hour?' It's my mother.

I overslept this morning, flung on a cardigan and got there just as everybody was standing up. It was Holy Communion so the militants were out in force, the sub-zero temperature in the side-chapel doubtless adding to the attraction.

Geoffrey kicks off by apologising for his failure to defrost the church. (Subdued merriment.) Mr Medlicott has shingles, Geoffrey explains, and, as is well known, has consistently refused to initiate us lesser mortals into the mysteries of the boiler. (Helpless laughter.)

Mrs Belcher read the lesson. Mr Belcher took the plate round. 'Big day for you,' I said to them afterwards.

The sermon was about sex. I didn't actually nod off, though I have heard it before. Marriage gives the OK to sex is the gist of it, but while it is far from being the be all and end all (you can say that again) sex is nevertheless the supreme joy of the married state and a symbol of the relationship between us and God. So, Geoffrey concludes, when we put our money in the plate it is a symbol of everything in our lives we are offering to God and that includes our sex. I could only find 10p.

Thinking about the sermon during the hymn I felt a pang of sympathy for the Deity, gifted with all this sex. No fun being made a present of the rare and desiccated conjunctions that take place between Geoffrey and me. Or the frightful collisions that presumably still occur between the Belchers. Not to mention whatever shamefaced fumblings go on between Miss Budd and Miss Bantock. 'It's all right if we offer it to God, Alice.' 'Well, if you say so, Pauline.'

Amazing scenes at the church door. Geoffrey had announced that after Easter the bishop would be paying us a visit so the fan club were running round in small circles, Miss Frobisher even going as far as to squeeze my elbow. Meanwhile, Geoffrey stands there the wind billowing out his surplice and ruffling his hair, what 'Who's Who in the Diocese of Ripon' calls 'his schoolboy good looks'. I helped put away the books while he did his 'underneath this cassock I am but a man like anybody else' act. 'Such a live wire,' said Mrs Belcher, 'really putting the parish on the map.' 'That's right,' burbles Mrs Shrubsole, looking at me. 'We must cherish him.'

We came back and I cherished him with some chicken wings in a tuna fish sauce. He said, 'That went down well.' I said, 'The chicken wings?' He said, 'My sermon. I felt it hit the nail on the head.' He put his hand over mine, hoping, I suppose, that having hit one nail he might hit another, but I said I had to go round with the parish magazine. 'Good girl,' he said. 'I can attack my paperwork instead.'

Roads busy. Sunday afternoon. Families having a run out. Wheeling the pram, walking the dog. Living. Almighty God unto whom all hearts be open, and from whom no secrets are hid, cleanse the thoughts of our hearts by the inspiration of thy holy spirit that we may perfectly love thee and worthily magnify thy glorious name and not spend our Sunday afternoons parked in a lay-by on the Ring Road wondering what happened to our life.

When I got back Geoffrey was just off to Evensong, was

I going to come? When I said 'No' he said, 'Really? Then I'd better pretend you have a headache.'

Why? One of the unsolved mysteries of life, or the unsolved mysteries of my life, is why the vicar's wife is expected to go to church at all. A barrister's wife doesn't have to go to court, an actor's wife isn't at every performance, so why have I always got to be on parade? Not to mention the larger question of whether one believes in God in the first place. It's assumed that being the vicar's wife one does but the question has never actually come up, not with Geoffrey anyway. I can understand why, of course. To look at me, the hair, the flat chest, the wan smile, you'd think I was just cut out for God. And maybe I am. I'd just like to have been asked that's all. Not that it matters of course. So long as you can run a tight jumble sale you can believe in what you like.

It could be that Geoffrey doesn't believe in God either. I've always longed to ask him only God never seems to crop up. 'Geoffrey,' I'd say. 'Yes, Susan?' 'Do you really believe in God? I mean, cards on tables, you don't honestly, do you? God's just a job like any other. You've got to bring home the bacon somehow.' But no. Not a word. The subject's never discussed.

After he'd gone I discovered we were out of sherry so I've just been round to the off-licence. The woman served me. Didn't smile. I can't think why. I spend enough.

GO TO BLACK.

Come up on Susan on the steps of the side-chapel, polishing a candlestick. Afternoon.

We were discussing the ordination of women. The bishop asked me what I thought. Should women take the services? So long as it doesn't have to be me, I wanted to say, they can be taken by a trained gorilla. 'Oh yes,' Geoffrey chips in, 'Susan's all in favour. She's keener than I am, aren't you, darling?' 'More sprouts anybody?' I said.

On the young side for a bishop, but he's been a prominent sportsman at university so that would explain it. Boxing or rugby. Broken nose at some stage anyway. One of the 'Christianity is common sense' brigade. Hobby's bricklaying apparently and refers to me throughout as 'Mrs Vicar'. Wants beer with his lunch and Geoffrey says he'll join him so this leaves me with the wine. Geoffrey's all over him because the rumour is he's shopping round for a new Archdeacon. Asks Geoff how outgoing I am. Actually says that. 'How outgoing is Mrs Vicar?' Mr Vicar jumps in with a quick rundown of my accomplishments and an outline of my punishing schedule. On a typical day, apparently, I kick off by changing the wheel on the Fiesta, then hasten to the bedside of a dying pensioner, after which, having done the altar flowers and dispensed warmth and appreciation to sundry parishioners en route, I top off a thrill-packed morning by taking round Meals on Wheels... somehow – 'and this to me is the miracle,' says Geoffrey – 'somehow managing to rustle up a delicious lunch in the interim', the miracle somewhat belied by the flabby lasagna we are currently embarked on. 'The ladies,' says the bishop. 'Where would we be without them?'

Disaster strikes as I'm doling out the tinned peaches: the jug into which I've decanted the Carnation milk gets knocked over, possibly by me. Geoffrey, for whom turning the other cheek is part of the job, claims it caught his elbow and his lordship takes the same line, insisting he gets doused in Carnation milk practically every day of his life. Still, when I get a dishcloth and sponge off his gaiters I catch him giving me a funny look. It's Mary Magdalene and the Nivea cream all over again. After lunch Geoffrey's supposed to be taking him on a tour of the parish but while we're having a cup of instant he claps his hand to his temple because he's suddenly remembered he's supposed to be in Keighley blessing a steam engine.

We're stacking the dishwasher and I ask Geoffrey how he thinks it's gone. Doesn't know. 'Fingers crossed,' I say. 'I think there are more constructive things we could do than that,' he says crisply, and goes off to mend his inner tube. I sit by the Aga for a bit and as I doze off it comes to me that by 'constructive things' he perhaps means prayer.

When I wake up there's a note from Geoffrey. 'Gone to talk to the Ladies Bright Hour. Go to bed.' I'm not sleepy and anyway we're running low on sherry so I drive into Leeds. I've stopped going round the corner now as I owe them a bit on the side and she's always so surly. There's a little Indian shop behind the Infirmary I've found. It's a newsagents basically but it sells drink and anything really, the way they do. Open last thing at night, Sundays included, my ideal. Ramesh he's called. Mr Ramesh I call him, though Ramesh may be his Christian name. Only not Christian of course. I've been once or twice now, only this time he sits me in the back place on a sack of something and talks. Little statuette of a god on the wall. A god. Not The God. Not the definite article. One of several thousand apparently. 'Safety in numbers,' I said but he didn't understand. Looks a bit more fun than Jesus anyway. Shows me pictures of other gods, getting up to all sorts. I said, 'She looks a very busy lady. Is that yoga?' He said, 'Well, it helps.' He's quite athletic himself apparently, married, but his wife's only about fourteen so they won't let her in. He calls me Mrs Vicar too, only it's different. He has lovely teeth.

GO TO BLACK.

Come up on Susan in the kitchen near the Aga. Morning.

Once upon a time I had my life planned out…or half of it at any rate. I wasn't clear about the first part, but at the stroke of fifty I was all set to turn into a wonderful woman…the wife to a doctor, or a vicar's wife, Chairman of the Parish Council, a pillar of the WI. A wise, witty and ultimately white-haired old lady, who's always stood on her own feet until one day at the age of eighty she comes out of the County Library, falls under the weight of her improving book, breaks her hip and dies peacefully, continently and without fuss under a snowy coverlet in the cottage hospital. And coming away from her funeral in a country churchyard on a bright winter's afternoon people would say, 'Well, she was a wonderful woman.'

Had this been a serious ambition I should have seen to it I was equipped with the skills necessary to its achievement. How to produce jam which, after reaching a good, rolling boil, successfully coats the spoon; how to whip up a Victoria sponge that just gives to the fingertips; how to plan, execute and carry through a successful garden fête. All weapons in the armoury of any upstanding Anglican lady. But I can do none of these things. I'm even a fool at the flower arrangement. I ought to have a PhD in the subject the number of classes I've been to but still my efforts show as much evidence of art as walking sticks in an umbrella stand. Actually it's temperament. I don't have it. If you think squash is a competitive activity try flower arrangement.

On this particular morning the rota has Miss Frobisher and Mrs Belcher down for the side aisles and I'm paired with Mrs Shrubsole to do the altar and the lectern. My honest opinion, never voiced needless to say, is that if they were really sincere about religion they'd forget flower arrangement altogether, invest in some permanent plastic jobs and put the money towards the current most popular famine. However, around mid-morning I wander over to the church with a few dog-eared chrysanthemums. They look as if they could do with an immediate drink so I call in at the vestry and root out a vase or two from the cupboard where Geoffrey keeps the communion wine.

It not looming very large on my horizon, I assume I am doing the altar and Mrs Shrubsole the lectern, but when I come out of the vestry Mrs S is at the altar well embarked on her arrangement. I said, 'I thought I was doing the altar.' She said, 'No. I think Mrs Belcher will bear me out. I'm down to do the altar. You are doing the lectern. Why?' She smiled sweetly. 'Do you have a preference?' The only preference I have is to shove my chrysanthemums up her nose but instead I practise a bit of Christian forbearance and go stick them in a vase by the lectern. In the best tradition of my floral arrangements they look like the poles of a wigwam, so I go and see if I can cadge a bit of backing from Mrs Belcher. 'Are you using this?' I say, picking up a bit of mouldy old fern. 'I certainly am. I need every bit of my spiraea. It gives it body.' I go over and see if Miss Frobisher has any greenery going begging only she's doing some Japanese number, a vase like a test-tube half filled with gravel, in which she's throttling a lone carnation. So I retire to the vestry for a bit to calm my shattered nerves, and when I come out ready to tackle my chrysanths again Mrs Shrubsole has apparently finished and fetched the other two up to the altar to admire her handiwork. So I wander up and take a look.

Well, it's a brown job, beech leaves, teazles, grass, that school of thought. Mrs Shrubsole is saying, 'It's called Forest Murmurs. It's what I did for my Highly Commended at Harrogate last year. What do you think?' Gert and Daisy are of course speechless with admiration, but when I tentatively suggest it might look a bit better if she cleared up all the bits and pieces lying around she said, 'What bits and pieces?' I said, 'All these acorns and fir-cones and whatnot. What's this conker in aid of?' She said, 'Leave that. The whole arrangement pivots on that.' I said, 'Pivots?' 'When the adjudicator was commenting on my arrangement he particularly singled out the hint I gave of the forest floor.' I said, 'Mrs Shrubsole. This is the altar of St Michael and All Angels. It is not The Wind in the Willows.' Mrs Belcher said, 'I think you ought to sit down.' I said, 'I do not want to sit down.' I said, 'It's all very well to transform the altar into something out of Bambi but do not forget that for the vicar the altar is his working surface. Furthermore,' I added, 'should the vicar sink to his knees in prayer, which since this is the altar he is wont to do, he is quite likely to get one of these teazle things in his eye. This is not a flower arrangement. It is a booby trap. A health hazard. In fact,' I say in a moment of supreme inspiration, 'it should be labelled HAZFLOR. Permit me to demonstrate.' And I begin getting down on my knees just to prove how lethal her bloody Forest Murmurs is. Only I must have slipped because next thing I know I'm rolling down the altar steps and end up banging my head on the communion rail.

Mrs Shrubsole, who along with every other organisation known to man has been in the St John's Ambulance Brigade, wants me left lying down, whereas Mrs Belcher is all for getting me on to a chair. 'Leave them lying down,' says Mrs Belcher, 'and they inhale their own vomit. It happens all the time, Veronica.' 'Only, Muriel,' says Mrs Shrubsole, 'when they have vomited. She hasn't vomited.' 'No,' I say, 'but I will if I have to listen to any more of this drivel,' and begin to get up. 'Is that blood, Veronica?' says Mrs Belcher pointing to my head. 'Well,' says Mrs Shrubsole, reluctant to concede to Mrs B on any matter remotely touching medicine, 'it could be, I suppose. What we need is some hot sweet tea.' 'I thought that theory had been discredited,' says Mrs Belcher. Discredited or not it sends Miss Frobisher streaking off to find a teabag, and also, it subsequently transpires, to telephone all and sundry in an effort to locate Geoffrey. He is in York taking part in the usual interdenominational conference on the role of the church in a hitherto uncolonised department of life, underfloor central heating possibly. He comes haring back thinking I'm at death's door, and finding I'm not has nothing more constructive to offer than I take a nap.

This gives the fan club the green light to invade the vicarage, making endless tea and the vicar his lunch and, as he puts it, 'spoiling him rotten'. Since this also licenses them to conduct a fact-finding survey of all the housekeeping arrangements or absence of same ('Where does she keep the Duroglit, Vicar?'), a good time is had by all. Meanwhile Emily Brontë is laid out on the sofa in a light doze.

I come round to hear Geoffrey saying, 'Mrs Shrubsole's going now, darling.' I don't get up. I never even open my eyes. I just wave and say, 'Goodbye, Mrs Shrubsole.' Only thinking about it as I drift off again I think I may have said, 'Goodbye, Mrs Subsoil.' Anyway I meant the other. Shrubsoil.

When I woke up it was dark and Geoffrey'd gone out.

I couldn't find a thing in the cupboard so I got the car out and drove into Leeds. I sat in the shop for a bit, not saying much. Then I felt a bit wanny and Mr Ramesh let me go into the back place to lie down. I must have dozed off because when I woke up Mr Ramesh has come in and started taking off his clothes. I said, 'What are you doing? What about the shop?' He said, 'Do not worry about the shop. I have closed the shop.' I said, 'It's only nine. You don't close till eleven.' 'I do tonight,' he said. I said, 'What's tonight?' He said, 'A chance in a million. A turn-up for the books. Will you take your clothes off please.' And I did.

GO TO BLACK.

Come up on Susan sitting in the vestry having a cigarette. Afternoon.

You never see pictures of Jesus smiling, do you? I mentioned this to Geoffrey once. 'Good point, Susan,' is what he said, which made me wish I'd not brought it up in the first place. Said I should think of Our Lord as having an inward smile, the doctrine according to Geoffrey being that Jesus was made man so he smiled, laughed and did everything else just like the rest of us. 'Do you think he ever smirked?' I asked, whereupon Geoffrey suddenly remembered he was burying somebody in five minutes and took himself off.

If Jesus is all man I just wish they'd put a bit more of it into the illustrations. I was sitting in church yesterday, wrestling with this point of theology, when it occurred to me that something seemed to have happened to Geoffrey. The service should have kicked off ages ago but he's still in the vestry. Mr Bland is filling in with something uplifting on the organ and Miss Frobisher, never one to let an opportunity slip, has slumped to her knees for a spot of unscheduled silent prayer. Mrs Shrubsole is lost in contemplation of the altar, still adorned with Forest Murmurs, a trail of ivy round the cross the final inspired touch. Mr Bland now ups the volume but still no sign of Geoff. 'Arnold,' says Mrs Belcher, 'there seems to be some hiatus in the proceedings,' and suddenly the fan club is on red alert. She's just levering him to his feet when I get in first and nip in there to investigate.

His reverence is there, white-faced, every cupboard open and practically in tears. He said, 'Have you seen it?' I said, 'What?' He said, 'The wine. The communion wine. It's gone.' I said, 'That's no tragedy,' and offer to pop out and get some ordinary. Geoffrey said, 'They're not open. Besides, what does it look like?' I said, 'Well, it looks like we've run out of communion wine.' He said, 'We haven't run out. There was a full bottle here on Friday. Somebody has drunk it.'

It's on the tip of my tongue to say that if Jesus is all he's cracked up to be why doesn't he use tap-water and put it to the test when I suddenly remember that Mr Bland keeps a bottle of cough mixture in his cupboard in case any of the choirboys gets chesty. At the thought of celebrating the Lord's Supper in Benylin Geoffrey now has a complete nervous breakdown but, as I point out, it's red and sweet and nobody is going to notice. Nor do they. I see Mr Belcher licking his lips a bit thoughtfully as he walks back down the aisle but that's all. 'What was the delay?' asks Mrs Shrubsole. 'Nothing,' I said, 'just a little hiccup.'

Having got it right for once I'm feeling quite pleased with myself, but Geoffrey obviously isn't and never speaks all afternoon so I bunk off Evensong and go into Leeds.

Mr Ramesh has evidently been expecting me because there's a bed made up in the storeroom upstairs. I go up first and get in. When I'm in bed I can put my hand out and feel the lentils running through my fingers. When he comes up he's put on his proper clothes. Long white shirt, sash and whatnot. Loincloth underneath. All spotless. Like Jesus. Only not. I watch him undress and think about them all at Evensong and Geoffrey praying in that pausy way he does, giving you time to mean each phrase. And the fan club lapping it up, thinking they love God when they just love Geoffrey. Lighten our darkness we beseech thee O Lord and by thy great mercy defend us from all perils and dangers of this night. Like Mr Ramesh who is twenty-six with lovely legs, who goes swimming every morning at Merrion Street Baths and plays hockey for Horsforth. I ask him if they offer their sex to God. He isn't very interested in the point but with them, so far as I can gather, sex is all part of God anyway. I can see why too. It's the first time I really understand what all the fuss is about. There among the lentils on the second Sunday after Trinity.

I've just popped into the vestry. He's put a lock on the cupboard door.

GO TO BLACK.

Come up on Susan sitting in the drawing-room of the vicarage. Much smarter than in previous scenes, she has had her hair done and seems a different woman. Evening.

I stand up and say, 'My name is Susan. I am a vicar's wife and I am an alcoholic.' Then I tell my story. Or some of it anyway. 'Don't pull any punches,' says Clem, my counsellor. 'Nobody's going to be shocked, believe me love, we've all been there.' But I don't tell them about Mr Ramesh because they've not been there. 'Listen, people. I was so drunk I used to go and sleep with an Asian grocer. Yes, and you won't believe this. I loved it. Loved every minute.' Dear oh dear. This was a real drunken lady.

So I draw a veil over Mr Ramesh who once, on the feast of St Simon and St Jude (Choral Evensong at six, daily services at the customary hour), put make-up on his eyes and bells on his ankles, and naked except for his little belt danced in the back room of the shop with a tambourine.

'So how did you come to AA?' they ask. 'My husband,' I say. 'The vicar. He persuaded me.' But I lie. It was not my husband, it was Mr Ramesh, the exquisitely delicate and polite Mr Ramesh who one Sunday night turned his troubled face towards me with its struggling moustache and asked if he might take the bull by the horns and enquire if intoxication was a prerequisite for sexual intercourse, or whether it was only when I was going to bed with him, the beautiful Mr Ramesh, twenty-six, with wonderful legs, whether it was only with him I had to be inebriated. And was it, asked this slim, flawless and troubled creature, was it perhaps his colour? Because if not he would like to float the suggestion that sober might be even nicer. So the credit for the road to Damascus goes to Mr Ramesh, whose first name turns out also to be Ramesh. Ramesh Ramesh, a member of the community council and the Leeds Federation of Trade.

But none of this I say. In fact I never say anything at all. Only when it becomes plain to Geoffrey (and it takes all of three weeks) that Mrs Vicar is finally on the wagon, who is it gets the credit? Not one of Mr Ramesh's jolly little gods, busy doing everything under the sun to one another, much like Mr Ramesh. Oh no. It's full marks to Geoffrey's chum, the Deity, moving in his well-known mysterious way.

So now everything has changed. For the moment I am a new woman and Geoffrey is a new man. And he brings it up on the slightest pretext. 'My wife's an alcoholic, you know. Yes. It's a great challenge to me and to the parish as extended family.' From being a fly in the ointment I find myself transformed into a feather in his cap. Included it in his sermon on Prayers Answered when he reveals that he and the fan club have been having these jolly get togethers in which they'd all prayed over what he calls 'my problem'. It practically sent me racing back to the Tio Pepe even to think of it. The fans, of course, never dreaming that their prayers would be answered, are furious. They think it's brought us closer together. Geoffrey thinks that too. We were at some doleful diocesan jamboree last week and I'm stuck there clutching my grapefruit juice as Geoffrey's telling the tale to some bearded cleric. Suddenly he seizes my hand. 'We met it with love,' he cries, as if love were some all-purpose antibiotic, which to Geoffrey it probably is.

And it goes on, the mileage in it endless. I said to Geoffrey that when I stood up at AA I sometimes told the story about the flower arranging. Result: he starts telling it all over the diocese. The first time was at a conference on The Supportive Parish. Gales of deep, liberated, caring laughter. He's now given it a new twist and tells the story as if he's talking about a parishioner, then at the end he says, 'Friends I want to tell you something. (Deep hush.) That drunken flower-arranger was my wife.' Silence…then the applause, terrific.

I've caught the other young, upwardly mobile parsons sneaking looks at me now and again and you can see them thinking why weren't they smart enough to marry an alcoholic or better still a drug addict, problem wives whom they could do a nice redemption job on, right there on their own doorstep. Because there's no stopping Geoffrey now. He grips my hand in public, nay brandishes it. 'We're a team,' he cries. Looks certain to be rural dean and that's only the beginning. As the bishop says, 'Just the kind of man we're looking for on the bench… someone with a seasoned compassion, someone who's looked life in the face. Someone who's been there.'

Mr Ramesh sold his shop. He's gone back to India to fetch his wife. She's old enough now apparently. I went down there on Sunday. There was a boy writing Under New Management on the window. Spelled wrong. And something underneath in Hindi, spelled right probably. He said he thought Mr Ramesh would be getting another shop, only in Preston.

They do that, of course, Asians, build something up, get it going nicely, then take the profit and move on. It's a good thing. We ought to be more like that, more enterprising.

My group meets twice a week and I go. Religiously. And that's what it is, of course. The names are different, Frankie and Steve, Susie and Clem. But it's actually Miss Frobisher and Mrs Shrubsole all over again. I never liked going to one church so I end up going to two. Geoffrey would call that the wonderful mystery of God. I call it bad taste. And I wouldn't do it to a dog. But that's the thing nobody ever says about God…he has no taste at all.

FADE OUT.

A LADY OF LETTERS

Irene Ruddock · Patricia Routledge

MISS RUDDOCK IS AN ORDINARY MIDDLE-AGED WOMAN. THE ROOM IN WHICH WE SEE HER IS SIMPLY FURNISHED AND THERE IS A BAY WINDOW. IT IS AFTERNOON.

I can't say the service was up to scratch. It smacked of the conveyor-belt. In fact I wrote to the crematorium. I said I thought the hallmark of a ceremony of that nature was reverence, whereas the word that kept coming into my mind was brisk. Moreover, I added, grief-stricken people do not expect to emerge from the Chapel of Rest to find grown men skulking in the rhododendrons with tab-ends in their mouths. If the hearse drivers must smoke then facilities should be provided. I'd heard good reports of this crematorium, but I hoped that they would agree with me that on this occasion it had let itself down.

Of course if I'd happened to be heartbroken I'd have felt much worse. I didn't let on to the crematorium because I thought it might get them off the hook but I actually didn't know her all that well. I used to see her getting on the 37 and we'd pass the time of day. She lost her mother round about the time I lost mine, she had a niece in Australia and I have the one cousin in Canada, then she went in for gas-fired central heating just a few weeks before I did, so one way and another we covered a lot of the same ground. I'd spent years thinking she was called Hammersley, which was way off the mark because her name turns out to be Pringle. There was a picture of her in the *Evening Post* (she'd been a big voluntary worker) with details of the funeral on the Wednesday afternoon, which is the one time I'm dangling my feet a bit, so I thought I'd get out my little maroon coat and put in an appearance. At least it's an outing. And I was glad I'd gone but, as I say, the ceremony was a bit lack-lustre and topped off by these young fellers smoking, so I thought the least I could do was write.

Anyway I had a charming letter back from the director of operations, a Mr Widdop. He said he was most grateful I'd drawn this matter to his attention and, while he was aware the practice sometimes went on, if he personally caught anybody smoking he would jump on the culprits with both feet. He knew I would appreciate that discipline within the chapel precincts presented special problems as it wasn't always convenient to tear a strip off somebody when there were grief-stricken people knocking about. What he personally preferred to do was to keep a low profile, then come down on the offenders like a ton of bricks once the coast was clear. With regard to my remarks about facilities, they had no plans to provide a smoking area in the Chapel of Rest in the foreseeable future as I must understand that space was at a premium and top of their list of priorities at the present moment was the provision of a temporary temple for the use of racial minorities. However, he would bear my remarks in mind, and if I were to come across any similar infringements in the future I was not to hesitate to get in touch.

I wrote him a little letter back thanking him for his prompt and courteous reply and saying that though I hoped not to be making any further visits to the crematorium in the near future (joke) I took his point. I also dropped a line to the relatives, care of the undertakers, saying that I was an acquaintance of Miss Pringle, had been present at the ceremony and had taken the liberty of entering into correspondence with the crematorium over the unfortunate lapse. I enclosed a copy of Mr Widdop's reply but they didn't write back, which I can understand because the one thing death always entails is a mass of correspondence. When Mother died I had fifty-three letters. Besides, they may not have even seen them smoking, they were probably blinded with grief. I see we've got a new couple moved in opposite. Don't look very promising. The kiddy looks filthy.

GO TO BLACK.

Come up on Miss Ruddock in the same setting. Morning.

A card from the opticians this morning saying that their records indicate that it's two years since they supplied me with spectacles and that by now they would almost certainly be in need of verification and suggesting I call at my earliest convenience. I thought that was nice so I took my trusty Platignum and dashed off an answer forthwith. I said I thought it was very considerate of them to have kept me in mind and while I was quite satisfied with my spectacles at the present moment I was grateful to them for drawing the matter to my attention and in the event of my noticing any deterioration I would in due course get in touch with them. (*She picks up her pen.*) It's stood me in good stead has this pen. Mother bought it me the last time she was able to get over to Harrogate. It's been a real friend. (*She glances in the direction of the window.*)

Angie her name is. I heard him shout of her as I went by en route for the Post Office. He was laid out underneath his car wanting a spanner and she came out, transistor in one hand, kiddy in the other. Thin little thing, bruise on its arm. I thought, 'Well, you've got a car, you've got a transistor, it's about time you invested in some curtains.' She can't be more than twenty and by the look of her she's expecting another.

I passed the place where there was the broken step I wrote to the council was a danger to the public. Little ramp there now, access for the disabled. Whenever I pass I think, 'Well, that's thanks to you, Irene.' My monument that ramp. Only some dog had gone and done its business right in the middle of it. I'm sure there's more of that than there used to be. I had a little Awayday to London last year and it was dog dirt everywhere. I spotted some on the pavement right outside Buckingham Palace. I wrote to the Queen about it. Had a charming letter back from a lady in waiting saying that Her Majesty appreciated my interest and that my letter had been passed on to the appropriate authority. The upshot eventually is I get a long letter from the chief cleansing officer to Westminster City Council apologising profusely and enclosing a rundown of their Highways and Maintenance Budget. That's been my experience generally...people are only too grateful to have these things pointed out. The keynote is participation. Of course I wrote back to thank him and then blow me if I didn't get another letter thanking me for mine. So I wrote back saying I hadn't been expecting another letter and there was no need to have written again and was this an appropriate use of public resources? They didn't even bother to reply. Typical.

Pause.

I'm just waiting for the paper coming. Not that there's much in it. The correspondence I initiated on the length of the Archbishop of Canterbury's hair seems to have gone off the boil. Till I wrote up to Live Letters nobody'd actually spotted it. Various people took up the cudgels until there was an impassioned letter from the Rural Dean of Halifax who has a beard and that seems to have put the tin hat on it.

Getting dark.

The couple opposite just having their tea. No cloth on. They must have put the kiddy to bed. When I put the milk bottle out I heard it crying.

GO TO BLACK.

Come up on Miss Ruddock sitting in an easy chair reading the newspaper. Afternoon.

Prison, they have it easy. Television, table tennis, art. It's just a holiday camp, do you wonder there's crime? And people say, 'Well, what can you do?' Well, you can get on to your MP for a start. I do, regularly. Got a reply to one letter this morning. I'd written drawing his attention to a hitherto unnoticed factor in the rise in crime, namely the number of policemen these days who wear glasses. What chance would they have against a determined assailant? He noted my comments and promised to make them known in the proper quarter. He's Labour but it's always very good notepaper and beautifully typed.

When I'd dusted round and done my jobs I had a walk on to the end and bought a little packet of pork sausage and some Basildon Bond. Big black hair in the sausage. So I wrote off to the makers enclosing the hair. Stuck it under a bit of Sellotape. Little arrow: 'This is the hair.' I emphasised that I didn't want a substitute packet, as it was plainly manufactured under unhygienic conditions, so would they send me a refund of the purchase price plus the cost of postage. I don't want inundating with sausage.

I keep wondering about the kiddy opposite. Haven't seen it for a week or two. And they're out all the time. Every single night they go off, and the kiddy doesn't go. And nobody comes in to sit. It can't be more than five. Where do they get the money to go out, that's what I'd like to know? Because he's not working. Spends all day tinkering with that car. There wants to be a bit less of the car and a bit more of the kiddy. It never plays out and they want fresh air do kiddies, it's a well-known fact. You don't hear it crying now, nothing. And I've never seen a cloth on. Teapot stuck there. Milk bottle. It'll surprise me if they're married. He has a tattoo anyway.

GO TO BLACK.

Come up on Miss Ruddock sitting on a dining chair in the window. Dusk.

My mother knew everybody in this street. She could reel off the occupants of every single house. Everybody could, once upon a time. Now, they come and they go. That's why these tragedies happen. Nobody watching. If they knew they were being watched they might behave. I'd talk to next door's about it only there hasn't been any contact since the business over the dustbins. And this other side's Asians so they won't know what's normal and what isn't. Though I've a feeling he's been educated and their kiddies are always beautifully turned out. I just wish they'd do something about their privet.

I thought I'd go and have a word with the doctor, drop a hint there somehow. There used to be just one doctor. Now they've all amalgamated so it's a bit of a lucky dip. Young fellow. I said I was getting upset, like I did before. 'Before what?' he said. I said, 'It's in my notes.' So he read them and then said, 'You've been getting a bit upset, like you did before.

I'll give you something to take.' So I told him about the kiddy, and he said, 'Well, these tablets will help you to take a more balanced view.' I gave them three or four days and they didn't seem to me to make much difference so I went along again. Different doctor this time. Same rigmarole. I said I didn't want any more tablets, I just wanted the name of the firm manufacturing the ones I'd already had, because I think they ought to be told if their product isn't doing the trick. The doctor said it would be easier if he gave me some new tablets and anyway I couldn't write, the firm was Swiss. I said, 'What difference does that make, everybody speaks English now.' He said, 'We don't want to get into that, do we?' and writes me another prescription. I shan't bother with it. In fact I put it down the toilet. I don't know who you write to about doctors.

After I'd had my tea I sat in the front room in the dark watching the house. He's messing about with the car, one of those little vests on they have now without sleeves. Radio going hammer and tongs. No kiddy still. I don't even know their name.

GO TO BLACK.

Come up on Miss Ruddock in her hat and coat against a bare background.

Thinking about it afterwards, I realised it must have been the doctor that alerted the vicar. Came round anyway. Not the old vicar. I'd have known him. This was a young fellow in a collar and tie, could have been anybody. I didn't take the chain off. I said, 'How do I know you're the vicar, have you any identification?' He shoves a little cross round the door. I said, 'What's this?' He said, 'A cross.' I said, 'A cross doesn't mean anything.

Youths wear crosses nowadays. Hooligans. They wear crosses in their ears.' He said, 'Not like this. This is a real cross. A working cross. It's the tool of my trade.' I was still a bit dubious, then I saw he had cycle clips on so I let him in.

He chats for a bit, this and that, no mention of God for long enough. They keep him up their sleeve for as long as they can, vicars, they know it puts people off. Went through a long rigmarole about love. How love comes in different forms... loving friends, loving the countryside, loving music. People would be surprised to learn, he said (and I thought, 'Here we go'), people would be surprised to learn that they loved God all the time and just didn't know it. I cut him short. I said, 'If you've come round here to talk about God you're barking up the wrong tree. I'm an atheist.' He was a bit stumped, I could see. They don't expect you to be an atheist when you're a miss. Vicars, they think if you're a single person they're on a good wicket. He said, 'Well, Miss Ruddock, I shall call again. I shall look on you as a challenge.'

He hadn't been gone long when there's another knock, only this time it's a policeman, with a woman policeman in tow. Ask if they can come in and have a word. I said, 'What for?' He said, 'You know what for.' I said, 'I don't,' but I let them in. Takes his helmet off, only young and says he'll come straight to the point: was it me who'd been writing these letters? I said, 'What letters? I don't write letters.' He said, 'Letters.' I said, 'Everyone writes letters. I bet you write letters.' He said, 'Not like you, love.' I said, 'Don't love me. You'd better give me your name and number. I intend to write to your superintendent.'

It turns out it's to do with the couple opposite. I said, 'Well, why are you asking me?' He said, 'We're asking you because who was it wrote to the chemist saying his wife was a prostitute? We're asking you because who was it gave the lollipop man a nervous breakdown?' I said, 'Well, he was interfering with those children.' He said, 'The court bound you over to keep the peace. This is a serious matter.' I said, 'It is a serious matter. I can't keep the peace when there's cruelty and neglect going on under my nose. I shouldn't keep the peace when there's a child suffering. It's not my duty to keep the peace then, is it?' So then madam takes over, the understanding approach. She said didn't I appreciate this was a caring young couple? I said if they were a caring young couple why did you never see the kiddy? If they were a caring young couple why did they go gadding off every night, leaving the kiddy alone in the house? She said because the kiddy wasn't alone in the house. The kiddy wasn't in the house. The kiddy was in hospital in Bradford, that's where they were going every night. And that's where the kiddy died, last Friday. I said, 'What of? Neglect?' She said, 'No. Leukaemia.'

Pause.

He said, 'You'd better get your hat and coat on.'

GO TO BLACK.

Come up on Miss Ruddock back at home. Day.

I've got two social workers come, one white, one black. Maureen I'm supposed to call the white one, shocking finger nails, ginger hair, and last week a hole in her tights as big as a 50p piece. She looks more in need of social work than I do. Puts it all down to men. 'We all know about men, don't we,

Irene.' I never said she could call me Irene. I don't want to be called Irene. I want to be called Miss Ruddock. I'm not Irene. I haven't been Irene since Mother died. But they all call me Irene, her, the police, everybody. They think they're being nice, only it's just a nice way of being nasty. The other one's Asian, Mrs Rabindi, little red spot on her forehead, all that. Sits, talks. She's right enough. Said I'd be useful in India. You can earn a living writing letters there apparently as they're all illiterate. Something daubed on her door last week. She says it's what you get to expect if you're Asian. I said, 'Well, there's all sorts gets chucked over my wall.' We sit and talk, only she's a bit of a boring woman. I tell her I loved my mother and she says how she loved her mother. I tell her I'm frightened to walk the streets and she tells me how she's been attacked herself. Well, it doesn't get you any further. It's all 'me too'. Social work, I think it's just chiming in.

I'm on what's called a suspended sentence. It means you have to toe the line. If I write any more letters I get sent to prison. The magistrate said I was more to be pitied than anything else. I said, 'Excuse me, could I interject?' He said, 'No. Your best plan would be to keep mum.' Big fellow, navy blue suit, poppy in his buttonhole. Looked a bit of a drinker.

Maureen says I should listen to local radio. Join these phone-in things. Chat to the disc jockey and choose a record. She says they're very effective in alleviating loneliness and a sense of being isolated in the community. I said, 'Yes and they're even more effective in bumping up the phone bill.' Maureen's trying to get me on reading. I suppose to get me off writing. She says books would widen my horizon. Fetches me novels, but they don't ring true. I mean, when somebody in a novel says something like 'I've never been in an air crash', you know this means that five minutes later they will be. Say trains never crash and one does. In stories saying it brings it on. So if you get the heroine saying, 'I don't suppose I shall ever be happy', then you can bank on it there's happiness just around the corner. That's the rule in novels. Whereas in life you can say you're never going to be happy and you never are happy, and saying it doesn't make a ha'porth of difference. That's the real rule. Sometimes I catch myself thinking it'll be better the second time round. (Pause.) But this is it. This has been my go.

Pause.

New policeman now. Walks the streets, the way they used to. Part of the new policy. Community policing. Smiles. Passes the time of day. Keeping an eye on things.

Certainly keeps an eye on No. 56. In there an hour at a stretch. Timed it the other day and when eventually he comes out she's at the door in just a little shorty housecoat thing.

He's in there now.

Pause.

He wants reporting.

GO TO BLACK.

Come up on Miss Ruddock against a plain institutional background. She is in a tracksuit, speaks very quickly and is radiant.

I ought to be writing up my diary. Mrs Proctor's got us all on keeping diaries as part of Literary Appreciation. The other girls can't think what to put in theirs, me I can't think what to leave out. Trouble is I never have time to write it up, I'm three days behind as it is.

I'm that busy. In a morning it's Occupation and I've opted for bookbinding and dressmaking. In dressmaking Mrs Dunlop's chucked me in at the deep end and I'm running up a little cocktail dress. I said, 'I never have cocktails.' She said, 'Well, now you've got the dress, you can.' That's what it's geared to, this place, new horizons. It's in shantung with a little shawl collar. Lucille's making me a chunky necklace for it in Handicrafts.

I share a room with Bridget, who's from Glasgow. She's been a prostitute on and off and did away with her kiddy, accidentally, when she was drunk and upset. Bonny little face, you'd never think it. Her mother was blind, but made beautiful pastry and brought up a family of nine in three rooms. You don't know you're born I think. I'm friends with practically everyone though besides Bridget. I'm up and down this corridor; more often than not I'm still on my rounds when the bell goes.

They laugh at me, I know, but it's all in good part. Lucille says, 'You're funny you, Irene. You don't mind being in prison.' I said, 'Prison!' I said, 'Lucille. This is the first taste of freedom I've had in years.'

Of course I'm lucky. The others miss the sex. Men, men, men. They talk about nothing else.

Mind you, that's not quite the closed book it used to be. Bridget's taken me through the procedure step by step and whereas previous to this if I'd ever found myself in bed with a man I should have been like a fish out of water, now, as Bridget says, at least I know the rudiments. Of course I can't ever see it coming to that at my age, but still it's nice to have another string to your bow. They've got me smoking now and again as well. I mean, I shan't ever be a full-time smoker, I'm not that type, and I don't want to be, but it means that if I'm ever in a social situation when I'm called on to smoke, like when they're toasting the Queen, I shan't be put off my stroke. But you see, that's the whole philosophy of this place: acquiring skills.

I sailed through the secretarial course, Miss Macaulay says I'm their first Grade I. I can type like the wind. Miss Macaulay says we mustn't let the grass grow under our feet and if she goes down on her knees in Admin they might (repeat might) let me have a go on their word processor. Then the plan is: Stage One, I go on day release for a bit, followed by Stage Two a spell in a resettlement hostel where I'll be reintegrated into the community. Then finally Stage Three a little job in an office somewhere. I said to Miss Macaulay, 'Will it matter my having been in prison?' She said, 'Irene, with your qualifications it wouldn't matter if you'd been in the SS.'

But the stuff some of them come out with! You have to smile. They have words for things I didn't know there were words for, and in fact I swear myself on occasion now, though only when the need arises. The other evening I'm sat with Shirley during Association. Shirley's very obese, I think it's glandular, and we're trying to put together a letter to her boy friend. Well, she says it's her boy friend only I had to start the letter three times because first go off she says his name's Kenneth, then she says it's Mark, and finally she settles on Stephen. She stammers does Shirley and I think she just wanted a name she could say. I don't believe she has a boy friend at all, just wants to be in the swim. She shouldn't actually be in here in fact, she's not all there but there's nowhere else to put her apparently, she sets fire to places. Anyway, we're sitting in her room concocting this letter to her pretend boy friend when Black Geraldine waltzes in and drapes herself across the bed and starts chipping in, saying was this boy friend blond, did he have curly hair, and then nasty personal-type questions she should know better than to ask Shirley. And Shirley's getting confused and stammering and Geraldine's laughing, so finally I threw caution to the winds and told Geraldine to fuck up.

She screams with laughing and goes running down the corridor saying, 'Do you know what Irene said, do you know what Irene said?' When she'd gone Shirley said, 'You shouldn't have said that.' I said, 'I know, but sometimes it's necessary.' She said, 'No, Irene. I don't mean you shouldn't have said it. Only you got it wrong. It's not fuck up.' I said, 'What is it?' She said, 'It's fuck off.' She's good-hearted.

Pause.

Sometimes Bridget will wake up in the middle of the night shouting, dreaming about the kiddy she killed, and I go over and sit by the bed and hold her hand till she's gone off again. There's my little clock ticking and I can hear the wind in the poplar trees by the playing field and maybe it's raining and I'm sitting there. And I'm so *happy*.

FADE OUT.

HER BIG CHANCE

Lesley · Julie Walters

LESLEY IS IN HER EARLY THIRTIES. SHE IS IN HER FLAT. MORNING.

I shot a man last week. In the back. I miss it now, it was really interesting. Still, I'm not going to get depressed about it. You have to look to the future. To have something like that under your belt can be quite useful, you never know when you might be called on to repeat the experience.

It wasn't in the line of duty. I wasn't a policewoman or someone who takes violence in their stride. It was with a harpoon gun actually, but it definitely wasn't an accident. My decision to kill was arrived at only after a visible tussle with my conscience. I had to make it plain that once I'd pulled the trigger things were never going to be the same again: this was a woman at the crossroads.

It wasn't *Crossroads*, of course. They don't shoot people in *Crossroads*, at any rate not with harpoon guns. If anybody did get shot it would be with a weapon more suited to the motel ambience. I have been in *Crossroads* though, actually. I was in an episode involving a fork lunch. At least I was told it was a fork lunch, the script said it was a finger buffet. I said to the floor manager, I said, 'Rex. Are you on cans because I'd like some direction on this point. Are we toying or are we tucking in?' He said, 'Forget it. We're losing the food anyway.' I was playing Woman in a Musquash Coat, a guest at a wedding reception, and I was scheduled just to be in that one episode. However in my performance I tried to suggest I'd taken a fancy to the hotel in the hope I might catch the director's eye and he'd have me stay on after the fork lunch for the following episode which involved a full-blown weekend. So I acted an interest in the soft furnishings, running my fingers over the Formica and admiring the carpet on the walls. Only Rex came over to say that they'd put me in a musquash coat to suggest I was a sophisticated woman, could I try and look as if I was more at home in a three star motel. I wasn't at home in that sort of motel I can tell you. I said to the man I'd been put next to, who I took to be my husband, I said, 'Curtains in orange nylon and no place mats, there's not even the veneer of civilisation.' He said, 'Don't talk to me about orange nylon. I was on a jury once that sentenced Richard Attenborough to death.' We'd been told to indulge in simulated cocktail chit-chat so we weren't being unprofessional, talking. That is something I pride myself on, actually: I am professional to my fingertips.

Whatever it is I'm doing, even if it's just a walk-on, I must must must get involved, right up to the hilt. I can't help it. People who know me tell me I'm a very serious person, only it's funny, I never get to do serious parts. The parts I get offered tend to be fun-loving girls who take life as it comes and aren't afraid of a good time should the opportunity arise-type-thing. I'd call them vivacious if that didn't carry overtones of the outdoor life. In a nutshell I play the kind of girl who's very much at home on a bar stool and who seldom has to light her own cigarette. That couldn't be more different from me because for a start I'm not a smoker. I mean, I can smoke if a part requires it. I'm a professional and you need as many strings to your bow as you can in this game. But, having said that, I'm not a natural smoker and what's more I surprise my friends by not being much of a party-goer either. (Rather curl up with a book quite frankly.) However, this particular party I'd made an exception. Thing was I'd met this ex-graphic designer who was quitting the rat race and going off to Zimbabwe and he was having a little farewell do in the flat of an air hostess friend of his in Mitcham, would I go? I thought, well it's not every day you get somebody going off to Zimbabwe, so I said 'Yes' and I'm glad I did because that's how I got the audition.

Now my hobby is people. I collect people. So when I saw this interesting-looking man in the corner, next thing is I find myself talking to him. I said, 'You look an interesting person. I'm interested in interesting people. Hello.' He said, 'Hello.' I said, 'What do you do?' He said, 'I'm in films.' I said, 'Oh, that's interesting, anything in the pipeline?' He said, 'As a matter of fact, yes,' and starts telling me about this project he's involved in making videos for the overseas market, targeted chiefly on West Germany. I said, 'Are you the producer?' He said, 'No, but I'm on the production side, the name's Spud.' I said, 'Spud! That's an interesting name, mine's Lesley.' He said, 'As it happens, Lesley, we've got a problem at the moment. Our main girl has had to drop out because her back's packed in. Are you an actress?' I said, 'Well, Spud, interesting that you should ask because as a matter of fact I am.' He said, 'Will you excuse me one moment, Lesley?' I said, 'Why, Spud, where are you going?' He said, 'I'm going to go away, Lesley, and make one phone call.'

It transpires the director is seeing possible replacements the very next day, at an address in West London. Spud said, 'It's interesting because I'm based in Ealing.' I said, 'Isn't that West London?' He said, 'It is. Where's your stamping ground?' I said, 'Bromley, for my sins.' He said, 'That's a far-ish cry. Why not bed down at my place?' I said, 'Thank you, kind sir, but I didn't fall off the Christmas tree yesterday.' He said, 'Lesley, I have a son studying hotel management and a daughter with one kidney. Besides, I've got my sister-in-law staying. She's come up for the Ideal Home Exhibition.'

The penny began to drop when I saw the tattoo. My experience of tattoos is that they're generally confined to the lower echelons, and when I saw his vest it had electrician written all over it. I never even saw the sister-in-law. Still traipsing round Olympia probably.

GO TO BLACK.

Come up on Lesley in the same setting. Afternoon.

I know something about personality. There's a chapter about it in this book I'm reading. It's by an American. They're the experts where personality is concerned, the Americans; they've got it down to a fine art. It makes a big thing of interviews so I was able to test it out.

The director's not very old, blue suit, tie loose, sleeves turned back. I put him down as a university type. Said his name was Simon, which I instantly committed to memory. (That's one of the points in the book: purpose and use of name.) He said, 'Forgive this crazy time.' I said, 'I'm sorry, Simon?' He said, 'Like 9.30 in the morning.' I said, 'Simon. The day begins when the day begins. You're the director.' He said, 'Yes, well. Can you tell me what you've done?'

I said, 'Where you may have seen me, Simon, is in *Tess*. Roman Polanski. I played Chloë.' 'I don't remember her,' he said. 'Is she in the book?' I said, 'Book? This is *Tess*, Simon. Roman Polanski. Chloë was the one on the back of the farm cart wearing a shawl. The shawl was original nineteenth-century embroidery. All hand done. Do you know Roman, Simon?' He said, 'Not personally, no.' I said, 'Physically he's quite small but we had a very good working relationship. Very open.' He said that was good, because Travis in the film was very open. I said, 'Travis? That's an interesting name, Simon.' He said, 'Yes. She's an interesting character, she spends most of the film on the deck of a yacht.' I said, 'Yacht? That's interesting, Simon. My brother-in-law has a small power boat berthed at Ipswich.' He said, 'Well! Snap!' I said, 'Yes, small world!' He said, 'In an ideal world, Lesley, I'd be happy to sit here chatting all day but I have a pretty tight schedule and, although I know it's only 9.30 in the morning, could I see you in your bra and panties?' I said, '9.30 in the morning, 10.30 at night, we're both professionals, Simon, but,' I said,'could we just put another bar on because if we don't you won't be able to tell my tits from goose-pimples.' He had to smile. That was another of the sections in the personality book: humour, usefulness of in breaking the ice.

When I'd got my things off he said, 'Well, you've passed the physical. Now the oral. Do you play chess?' I said, 'Chess, Simon? Do you mean the musical?' He said, 'No, the game.' I said, 'As a matter of fact, Simon, I don't. Is that a problem?' He said, 'Not if you water-ski. Travis is fundamentally an outdoor girl, but we thought it might be fun to make her an intellectual on the side.' I said, 'Well, Simon, I'm very happy to learn both chess and water-skiing, but could I make a suggestion? Reading generally indicates a studious temperament and I'm a very convincing reader,' I said, 'because it's something I frequently do in real life.' I could tell he was impressed. And so I said, 'Another suggestion I could make would be to kit Travis out with some glasses. Spectacles, Simon. These days they're not unbecoming and if you put Travis in spectacles with something in paperback, that says it all.' He said, 'You've been most helpful.' I said, 'The paperback could be something about the environment or, if you want to maintain the water-skiing theme, something about water-skiing and the environment possibly. I mean, Lake Windermere.'

He was showing me out by this time but I said, 'One last thought, Simon, and that is a briefcase. Put Travis in a bikini and give her a briefcase and you get the best of every possible world.' He said, 'I'm most grateful. You've given me a lot of ideas.' I said, 'Goodbye, Simon. I hope we can work together.' The drill for saying goodbye is you take the person's hand and then put your other hand over theirs, clasp it warmly while at the same time looking into their eyes, smiling and reiterating their name. This lodges you in their mind apparently. So I did all that, only going downstairs I had another thought and I popped back. He was on the phone. 'You won't believe this,' he was saying. I said, 'Don't hang up, Simon, only I just wanted to make it crystal clear that when I said briefcase I didn't mean the old-fashioned type ones, there are new briefcases now that open up and turn into a mini writing-desk. Being an up-to-the-minute girl, that would probably be the kind of briefcase Travis would have. She could be sitting in a wet bikini with a briefcase open on her knee. I've never seen that on screen so it would be some kind of first. Ciao, Simon. Take care.'

Pause.

That was last Friday. The book's got charts where you check your interview score. Mine was 75. Very good to excellent. Actually, I'm surprised they haven't telephoned.

GO TO BLACK.

Come up on Lesley, who is now made up and her hair done, sitting in a small bleak room in her dressing-gown. Morning.

You'd never think this frock wasn't made for me. I said to Scott, who's Wardrobe, 'She must be my double.' He said, 'No. You're hers. The stupid cow.'

Talk about last-minute, though. Eleven o'clock on Tuesday night I'm just wondering about having a run round with the dustette, six o'clock next morning I'm sitting in Lee-on-Solent in make-up. When the phone went telling me I'd got the part I assumed it was Simon. So I said, 'Hello Simon.' He said, 'Try Nigel.' So I said, 'Well, Nigel, can you tell Simon that I haven't let the grass grow under my feet. I now play a rudimentary game of chess.' He said, 'I don't care if you play a championship game of ice hockey, just don't get pregnant.'

It transpires the girl they'd slated to do the part had been living with a racing driver and of course the inevitable happened, kiddy on the way. So my name was next out of the hat. I said to Scott, 'I know why. They knew I had ideas about the part.' He said, 'They knew you had a 38-inch bust.' His mother's confined to a wheelchair, he's got a lot on his plate.

Anyway, I'm ready. I've been ready since yesterday morning. It was long enough before anybody came near. I had a bacon sandwich which Scott went and fetched for me while I was under the dryer. I said, 'Wasn't there a croissant?' He said, 'In Lee-on-Solent?' On *Tess* there were croissants. On *Tess* there was filter coffee. There was also some liaison.

I wanted to talk to somebody about the part, only Scott said they were out in the speed boat doing mute shots of the coastline. On *Tess* you were never sitting around. Roman anticipated every eventuality. We filmed in the middle of a forest once and the toilet arrangements were immaculate. There was also provision for a calorie-controlled diet. I said to Scott, 'I'm not used to working like this.' He said, 'Let's face it, dear. You're not used to working. Why didn't you bring your knitting?' I said, 'I do not knit, Scott.' He said, 'Well, file your nails then, pluck an eyebrow, be like me, do something constructive.' He's as thin as a rail and apparently an accomplished pianist and he seems to be make-up as well as wardrobe. On *Tess* we had three caravans for make-up alone.

Eventually Simon puts his head round the door. I said, 'Hello, Simon.' I said, 'Long time no see. Did Nigel tell you I've learned chess?' He said, 'Chess? Aren't you the one who can water-ski?' I said 'No.' He said 'Bugger' and disappeared. I said to Scott, 'Simon's on the young side for a director.' He said, 'Director? He couldn't direct you to the end of the street. He just does all the running about.' I said, 'Who is the director?' He said, 'Gunther.' I said, 'Gunther? That sounds a continental name.' He said, 'Yes. German.' I said, 'That's interesting. I went to Germany once. Dusseldorf.' He said, 'Well, you'll have a lot to talk about.' I've a feeling Scott may be gay. I normally like them only I think he's one of the ones it's turned bitter.

I'm still sitting there hours later when this other young fellow comes in. I said, 'Gunther?' He said, 'Nigel.' I said, 'We spoke on the phone.' He said, 'Yes. I'm about to commit suicide. I've just been told. You don't water-ski.' I said, 'Nigel. I could learn. I picked up the skateboard in five minutes.' He said, 'Precious. Five minutes is what we do not have. You don't by any chance have fluent French?' I said, 'No, why?' He said, 'They'd wondered about making her French.' I said, 'Nigel. How can she be French when she's called Travis? Travis isn't a French name.' He said, 'The name isn't important.' I said, 'It is to me. It's all I've got to build on.' He said, 'I'll get back to you.' I said, 'Nigel. I don't have French but what I do have is a smattering of Spanish, the legacy of several non-package type holidays on the Costa del Sol. Could Travis be half Spanish?' He said to Scott, 'We wanted someone with fluent French who could water-ski. What have we got? Someone with pidgin Spanish who plays chess.' Scott said, 'Well, don't tell me. I started off a landscape gardener.'

I was still waiting to be used in the afternoon which is when they did the water-skiing. Some girl from the local sub-aqua did it. She works part-time in the quayside restaurant where they all ate last night apparently. I saw her when she came in for make-up. Pleasant enough but didn't look a bit like me. I'm quite petite, only she was on the large side and whereas my hair is auburn hers was definitely ginger. I didn't say anything at the time but I thought if she's supposed to be me they'll be into big continuity problems so I thought I'd go in quest of the director and tell him. Nobody about on the yacht except a man who's dusting the camera. He said not to worry, the shot was p.o.v. water-skis so we'd only be seeing her elbow. I said, 'Will that work?' He said, 'Oh yes. You know, Cinema, the magic of.' Mind you, he said, if it was up to him personally, he'd rather see my elbow than hers any day. His name was Terry, what was mine? I said, 'It's a relief to find someone civil.' He said, 'It's the usual story, Lesley, Art comes in at the door, manners go out of the window. Why is making a film like being a mushroom?'

I said, 'Why, Terry?' He said, 'They keep you in the dark and every now and again somebody comes and throws a bucket of shit over you.' He laughed. I said, 'That's interesting, only Terry, they don't grow mushrooms like that now. It's all industrialised.' He said, 'You sound like a cultured person, what say we spend the evening exploring the delights of Lee-on-Solent?'

His room's nicer than mine. His bathroom's got a hair-dryer.

GO TO BLACK.

Come up on Lesley now in a bikini and wrap. An anonymous hotel room. Evening.

Please don't misunderstand me. I've no objection to taking my top off. But Travis as I was playing her wasn't the kind of girl who would take her top off. I said, 'I'm a professional, Nigel. Credit me with a little experience. It isn't Travis.'

I'd been sitting on the deck of the yacht all day as background while these two older men had what I presumed was a business discussion. One of them, who was covered in hair and had a real weight problem, was my boy friend apparently. You knew he was my boy friend because at an earlier juncture you'd seen him hit me across the face. Travis is supposed to be a good-time girl, though you never actually see me having a good time, just sat on this freezing cold deck plastering on the sun tan lotion. I said to Nigel, 'I don't know whether the cameraman's spotted it, Nigel, but would I be sunbathing? There's no sun.' Nigel said, 'No sun is favourite.' Nigel's first assistant, here there and everywhere. Gunther never speaks, not to me anyway. Just stands behind the camera with a little cap on. Not a patch on Roman. Roman had a smile for everybody.

Anyway, I'm sitting there as background and I say to Nigel, 'Nigel, am I right in thinking I'm a denizen of the cocktail belt?' He said, 'Why?' a bit guardedly. I said, 'Because to me, Nigel, that implies a cigarette-holder,' and I produced quite a modest one I happened to have brought with me. He went and spoke to Gunther, only Gunther ruled there was to be no smoking. I said, 'On grounds of health?' Nigel said, 'No. On grounds of it making continuity a bugger.' I'd also brought a paperback with me just to make it easier for props (which seemed to be Scott again). Only I'd hardly got it open when Nigel relieved me of it and said they were going for the sun tan lotion. I said, 'Nigel, I don't think the two are incompatible. I can apply sun tan lotion and read at the same time. That is what professionalism means.' He checked with Gunther again and he came back and said, 'Forget the book. Sun tan lotion is favourite.' I said, 'Can I ask you something else?' He said, 'Go on.' I said, 'What is my boy friend discussing?' He said, 'Business.' I said, 'Nigel. Would I be right in thinking it's a drugs deal?' He said, 'Does it matter?' I said, 'It matters to me. It matters to Travis. It helps my character.' He said, 'What would help your character is if you took your bikini top off.' I said, 'Nigel. Would Travis do that?' I said, 'We know Travis plays chess. She also reads. Is Travis the type to go topless?' He said, 'Listen. Who do you think you're playing, Emily Brontë? Gunther wants to see your knockers.'

I didn't even look at him. I just took my top off without a word and applied sun tan lotion with all the contempt I could muster. They did the shot, then Nigel came over and said Gunther liked that and if I could give him a whisker more sensuality it might be worth a close-up. So we did it again and then Nigel came over and said Gunther was liking what I was giving them and in this next shot would I slip off my bikini bottom. I said, 'Nigel. Trust me. Travis would not do that.' Talks to Gunther. Comes back. Says Gunther agrees with me. The real Travis wouldn't. But by displaying herself naked before her boy friend's business associate she is showing her contempt for his whole way of life. I said, 'Nigel. At last Gunther is giving me something I can relate to.' He says, 'Right! Let's shoot it! Elbow the bikini bottom!'

Pause.

We wrapped about six (that's film parlance for packed up). I said to Nigel, 'Did I give Gunther what he wanted? Is he happy?' He said, 'Gunther is an artist, Lesley. He's never happy. But as he said this afternoon, "At last we're cooking with gas."' I said, 'Does that mean it's good?' He said, 'Yes.' I said, 'Oh. Because I prefer electricity.'

When I got back to the hotel, it took me some time to unwind. I'd become so identified with Travis it was only when I'd had a bath and freshened up I felt her loosening her hold on me. I was looking forward to relaxing with the crew, swapping anecdotes of the day's shooting in the knowledge of a day's work well done only when I got downstairs there was nobody about, just Scott and one of the drivers. Turns out all the rest of them had gone off to supper at the restaurant run by the fat girl who did the water-skiing.

I sat in the bar for a bit. Just one fellow in there. I said, 'My hobby is people, what do you do?' Lo and behold he's on the film too, the animal handler, Kenny. In charge of the cat. I said, 'That's interesting, Kenny. I didn't know there was going to be a cat. I love cats. I love dogs too, but I love cats.' He said, 'Would you care to see her? She's asleep on my bed.' I said, 'That's convenient.' He said, 'Lesley. Don't run away with that idea. I am wedded to my small charges.' So I go up and pal on with the cat a bit and Kenny tells me about all the animals he's handled, a zebra once, a seal, an alligator and umpteen ferrets.

He has a trout there too in a tank. It was going to be caught later on in the film. Quite small, only they were going to shoot it in close-up so it would look bigger.

I sat on the bed and listened to him talk about animal behaviour. I said, 'Kenny, this is the kind of evening I like, two people just talking about something interesting.'

I woke up in the night and couldn't remember where I was. Then I saw the cat sitting there, watching the trout.

GO TO BLACK.

Come up on Lesley back in her own flat and in her ordinary clothes. Dusk.

When you've finished a shot on a film you have to wait and see whether there's what they call a hair in the gate. It's film parlance for the all clear. Thank God there wasn't because I couldn't have done it again. I'd created Travis and though it was her lover that got shot I felt it was the something in me that was Travis that had died.

My lover's name turned out to be Alfredo. That was my big line. 'Alfredo!' He was the head of some sort of crime syndicate only everybody in the yachting fraternity thought he was very respectable and to do with the building trade. One night while Alfredo and me were ashore at a building federation dinner and dance this young undercover policeman swims out to the yacht to search it in his underpants. However, as luck would have it Travis has a headache, so she and Alfredo return early from this ultra-respectable function with Alfredo in a towering rage. Originally I was down to say, 'I can't help it, Alfredo, I have a headache,' and we tried it once or twice only

Gunther then thought it would be more convincing if my headache was so bad I couldn't actually speak and Alfredo just said, 'You and your headaches.' I said, 'If it's a migraine rather than a headache Travis probably wouldn't be able to speak,' and Gunther said, 'Whatever you say.' It's wonderful, that moment, when you feel a director first begin to trust you and you can really start to build.

Anyway Travis and Alfredo come into the cabin where they find this young man behind the sofa in his underpants and Alfredo takes out his gun and says, 'How lucky lovely Travis had a headache and we had to leave our glittering reception. I was cross with her then but now my mood has changed. Offer the gentleman a drink, Travis. Then go and take your clothes off. There's nothing I like better than making love after killing a policeman. Ha ha.' I then retire to the next cabin while Alfredo taunts this bare young policeman and says he is going to kill him, but before he does so, he tells him about his drug-smuggling operation in every detail, the way criminals tend to do the minute they get somebody at gunpoint. When Travis comes back with no clothes on the young policeman is talking about the evil drugs do, all the young lives ruined and so on. Only I forgot to say that there'd been some dialogue earlier, when I was supposed to be snorkelling, about how Travis had a little brother, Craig, and how he'd got hooked on drugs and how I was heartbroken and determined to revenge myself on the culprits should I ever come across them.

So when the policeman is saying all this about the horror of drugs you can see it comes as a revelation to Travis that her lover is involved in drugs: she thinks it's just been ordinary crime and stealing electrical goods. Anyway very quietly, 'almost pensively' Gunther said, Travis picks up an underwater spear gun that happens to be on the sideboard. Nigel came over and said that ideally at this point Gunther would like to see a variety of emotions chase themselves across Travis's face as her affection for her lover, Alfredo, fights with the demands of her conscience and the memories of her little brother, Craig. You see my lover's fat finger tighten on the trigger as he gets ready to shoot the policeman, only just then I say his name very quietly, 'Alfredo'. He spins round. Travis fires the harpoon and you see the spear come out of his back, killing him, and also ruining his dinner jacket. They then follow that with a big close-up with blood and everything, and me with a single tear rolling down my cheek.

We did this in one take, which Nigel said was almost unique in the annals of filming. Only Scott has to chip in and say good job, as just having one dinner jacket was fairly unique as well. I couldn't have done it again anyway. I'd got nothing left. Except I suddenly had a flash of inspiration, the way you do when you've been to the end of the world and back, and I said to Nigel, 'Don't you think that Travis, drained of all emotion by the death of her lover, would perhaps cling on to the policeman whose life she has saved, and that they would celebrate his deliverance by having sexual intercourse there and then?'

Big debate. Gunther really liked it, only the actor playing the policeman wasn't keen. I think he may have been gay too, he had a moustache. Eventually Nigel came over and said that favourite was for the policeman to look as if he was considering having sexual intercourse and for him to run his hand speculatively over Travis's private parts, only then pity drives out lust and instead he covers up her nakedness with an oriental-type dressing-gown, the property of her dead lover.

Though even at this late stage you can tell he's not ruled out the possibility because as he's fastening the dressing-gown his fingers linger over Travis's nipples. Afterwards Gunther explained that if there had been any proper funny business at this point it would have detracted from the final scene when after all the excitement the undercover policeman goes home to his regular girl friend, who cooks him a hot snack and who's a librarian, and then the final scene is of them making love, the message being that sexual intercourse is better with someone you're in love with even though they are a bit homely and work in the county library than with someone like Travis who's just after a good time. As Gunther said to me that night, 'It's a very moral film only the tragedy is, people won't see it.' I said to him, I said, 'That's interesting because I saw it that way right from the start.'

When we were in bed I said, 'If only we could have done this before.' He said, 'Lesley. I make it a rule never to lay a finger on an actress until the whole thing's in the can.' I said, 'Gunther. There's no need to explain. We're both professionals. But Gunther,' I said, 'can I ask you one question? Was I Travis? Were you pleased with my performance?' He said, 'Listen. If someone is a bad actress I can't sleep with her. So don't ask me if I was pleased with your performance. This is the proof.' He's a real artist is Gunther.

When I woke up in the morning he'd gone. I wandered down for some coffee only there was nobody from the unit about. I'd planned to say goodbye to everybody but they were off doing some establishing shots of the marina. Anyway, I went and bought a card with a sinking ship on it and put 'Goodbye, gang! See you at the première!' and left it at the desk.

As I came out with my bags Scott was just loading the

laundry. I said, 'Ciao, Scott. It's been a pleasure working with you.' He said, 'You win some, you lose some.' I said, 'Now it's back to real life.' He said, 'Some of us never left it.' It's funny the way their clothes are always too small.

The film's coming out in West Germany initially, then Turkey possibly. Gunther says it'll make me quite famous. Well, I suppose I shall have to live with that. Only I'm not just going to sit here and wait for the phone to ring. No fear. I'm going to acquire another skill. Spoken Italian. Selling valuable oil paintings. Canoeing. You see, the more you have to offer as a person the better you are as an actress. Acting is really just giving.

FADE OUT.

SOLDIERING ON

Muriel · Stephanie Cole

MURIEL IS A BRISK, SENSIBLE WOMAN IN HER LATE FIFTIES. SHE IS IN A TWEED SKIRT AND CARDIGAN WITH SOME PEARLS, AND WE COME ON HER SETTLED IN A CORNER OF HER COMFORTABLE HOME. IT IS AFTERNOON.

It's a funny time, three o'clock, too late for lunch but a bit early for tea. Besides, there were one or two brave souls who'd trekked all the way from Wolverhampton; I couldn't risk giving them tea or we'd have had a mutiny on our hands. And I think people like to be offered something even if they don't actually eat it. One's first instinct was to make a beeline for the freezer and rout out the inevitable quiche, but I thought, 'Muriel, old girl, that's the coward's way out,' so the upshot was I stopped up till two in the morning trundling out a selection of my old standards... chicken in a lemon sauce, beef en croute from the old Colchester days (I thought of Jessie Marchant), and bushels of assorted salads. As it happened it wasn't exactly a salady day, quite crisp for April actually, however Mabel warmed up the proceedings with one of her famous soups, conjured up out of thin air, so we lived to fight another day. Nobody could quite put their finger on the flavour, so I was able to go round saying, 'Have you guessed the soup yet?' and that broke the ice a bit. I don't know what had got into Mabel but she'd gone mad and added a pinch of curry and that foxed most people. It was cauliflower actually.

Still, it was a bit sticky at the start as these occasions generally are. There were people there one didn't know from Adam (all the Massey-Ferguson people for instance, completely unknown quantities to me), and then lots of people I knew I should know and didn't. But whenever I saw anyone looking lost I thought of Ralph and grabbed hold of someone I did know and breezed up saying, 'This is Jocelyn. She's at the Royal College of Art. I don't know your name but the odds are you're in agricultural machinery,' and then left them to it. It was a case of light the blue touch paper and retire.

Knowing Ralph, of course, it was a real mixed bag. Several there from the Sports Council and quite a contingent from Tonbridge, some Friends of Norwich Cathedral and the Discharged Prisoners Aid Society, Madge and Perce whom we met on the *Mauretania* on our honeymoon, Donald and Joyce Bannerman who were actually en route for Abu Dhabi, then Donald bought a paper at Heathrow, saw the announcement and came straight down. And one sweet old man who'd come all the way over from Margate. He said, 'You won't remember me, Mrs Carpenter, but I'm a member of the criminal fraternity.' I shrieked. As the vicar said: Ralph touched life at many points.

The children magnificent, of course, or Giles at any rate. Luckily Margaret didn't appear. But Giles took off all the Household Brigade people on a tour of the garden while Pippa coped with some of the bigwigs from the City. 'I don't think you know George,' I heard one of them say, 'George cracks the whip at Goodison, Brown.' Poor souls, they both of them deserved medals. And Crispin and Lucy angelic, Crispin popping in and out of people's legs reaching up to fill the glasses. I wanted them to have a rest. 'No,' said Giles, 'let them do it. They adored their grandpa.' 'Adored him,' said Pippa, 'like we all did.'

The church had been absolutely chocker and I'd managed not to blub until right at the finish when they struck up with 'I vow to thee my country'. And then I'd a hundred and one things to do so I was perfectly all right until I saw awful Angela Gillespie had made the mistake of talking to boring old Frank from the firm, and I heard the dreaded words 'fork-lift trucks' and thought how many times I used to have to shut Ralph up in similar circumstances, and the idea of shutting Ralph up at all set me off instantly and I had to nip into the pantry to staunch the flow, shortly to be followed by Mabel who'd just fallen over one of his old wellingtons and promptly gone into floods. So we had a good laugh and a good cry over that before powdering our noses and hurling ourselves back into the fray.

When everybody'd gone I'm just having five minutes in the chair before tackling the debris when Margaret comes plunging into the room. She said, 'What were all those people?' I said, 'It was a kind of party for Daddy.' She said, 'Why? Is he dead?' I said, 'You know he's dead.' She said, 'Who killed him?' I said, 'Don't be such a donkey. Come along and we'll find you a tablet.' Some of Ralph's medicine's still in the cupboard. Fat lot of good that did, I thought, and poured it down the lav. Then felt a bit choked.

Anyway the tablet did the trick. I heard her walking about at two in the morning but I didn't get up. Except then I had to get up anyway because it suddenly came to me, in all the excitement I'd completely forgotten to feed the dogs.

GO TO BLACK.

Come up on Muriel sitting in an armchair. Evening.

Everybody I run into says not to take any big decisions. I staggered into the Community Centre bearing Ralph's entire wardrobe which Angela Gillespie had nipped in smartish and earmarked for Muscular Dystrophy. Five minutes later, Brenda Bousfield had come knocking at the door on behalf of Cystic

Fibrosis. Knives out straightaway, I practically had to separate them. In fact I did separate them in the end, the City suits to Angela and Brenda the tweeds. All lovely stuff. Beautiful dinner jacket from Hawes and Curtis, done for Giles if he hadn't got so fat. Mind you, he didn't want the ties either. Angela did. 'Lovely jumble,' she said. 'How're you coping? Don't take any big decisions, one day at a time, I don't see any shoes.'

Actually I'd been silly and kept his shoes back. I loved his shoes. Always used to clean them. 'My shoeshine lady.' 'Whatever you do,' Angela said, 'don't give them to Brenda. They're top-heavy on staff, their group, it's well known. It all goes on the admin. We can use shoes.'

I thought I'd go into the library and see if Miss Dunsmore could find me something on bereavement. That's something I learned from Ralph: plug into other people's experience, pool your resources. 'A new experience is like travelling through unknown country. But remember, others have taken this road before you, old girl, and left notes. So Question no. 1: Is there a map? Question no. 2: Am I taking advantage of all the information available? It doesn't matter if you're going to get married, commit a burglary or keep a guinea pig; efficiency is the proper collation of information.' Oh Ralph.

Miss Dunsmore did a reconnoitre round, but the only information she could come up with was a book about burial customs in Papua New Guinea. I think even Ralph would draw the line at that. However, she thought the Health Centre did a pamphlet on bereavement. Miss Dunsmore said she wasn't offering this as consolation but apparently elephants go into mourning and so, very strangely, does the pike. So we chatted about that for a bit. Told me not to take any big decisions, and if I was throwing away any of his books could I steer them her way as she ran some sort of reading service for the disabled.

I dropped into the Health Centre and the receptionist said there was a pamphlet on death; they'd had some on the counter, only the tots kept taking them to scribble on, so they hadn't re-ordered. She said she'd skimmed through it and the gist of it was not to take any big decisions and to throw yourself into something. I said, 'You don't mean the canal?' She said, 'Come again?' Nobody expects you to make jokes. As I was going out she called me back and said did Ralph wear spectacles? Because if he did, not to throw away the old pairs as owing to cutbacks they'd started a spectacles recycling scheme.

Back at base Mabel said Margaret had been plonked on the chair in the passage all morning with her bag packed and her outside coat on, and for some reason wellington boots. Said the police were coming. We manhandled her upstairs, and after about seventeen goes I managed to smuggle in a tablet which did the trick and she'd just settled down for a little zizz when who should draw up at the door but Giles.

He'd cancelled all his appointments, eluded the guards at the office and just belted down the A12 because he suddenly thought I might need cheering up, bless him. He could always get round Mabel ever since he was little, so she agrees to hold the fort while he whisks me off to lunch at somewhere rather swish. I thought to myself, I hope you're watching, Ralph, you old rascal, and eating your words. Ralph and Giles never got on for more than five minutes whereas, it's funny, he was always dotty about Mags.

When eventually we get back, what with all the wine etc. (I mean pudding *and* cheese), I'm just longing to put my head down, but Giles cracks the whip and gets me to sign lots of papers. It turns out Ralph's left me very nicely off. What with the house and all his various holdings, one way and another I'm quite a rich lady. He's tied a bit up for Margaret, nothing specific for Giles, but he doesn't mind because of course he doesn't need any and when I go he'll get it all anyway. But what I do have is what Giles calls a liquidity problem, and the first item on the agenda is to give me some ready cash, hence the papers. Then something about buying a forest. Bit wary to start with, said, 'Can I not mull it?' and Giles said, 'Well you can, but the index is going down.' I said, 'What about Mr Sherlock?' Giles said, 'You know what lawyers are.' Wish old Ralph could have seen me, signing away. He never showed me any papers at all, whereas Giles took me through them and explained it all. I suppose it's a different generation. What he did do, which made me feel a tiny bit shifty, was to take away three or four of the best pictures, the two carriage clocks and a couple of other choice items. Said that when the sharks from the revenue came round to assess the stuff for estate duty these were just the items that would bump the figure up. I said, 'What about the inventory?' Giles said, 'I think we'll just drag our brogues on that one.' Apparently everybody does it. He's just going to keep the stuff under the bed at Sloane Street until the heat is off, then back they come.

Margaret still lying on the bed when I went upstairs. Asleep she looks quite presentable. Daddy's little girl. Not so little now, those great legs. But as Mabel says, 'It looks as if we're on the hospital trail again.' If she goes in, I could perhaps go to Siena. Except I've nobody to go with. One keeps forgetting that.

GO TO BLACK.

Come up on Muriel sitting at a table writing letters. Afternoon.

It's not an ideal place, no one is saying it is. Even Giles doesn't say that. In fact it's a perfect example of one of those places they're always famously about to scrap. Started life as a workhouse probably, during the Napoleonic Wars, and *qua* building not displeasing. As someone weaned on Nikolaus Pevsner and practically a founder member of the National Trust I wouldn't alter a single brick. And as an arts centre first rate. As a museum of industrial archaeology...couldn't be bettered. Or as a craft centre, weaving, pottery, a shop-window where craftsmen and craftswomen could make and display their wares...absolutely ideal, the very place. But as a mental hospital...oh no, no, no, no, no.

The food, for instance. The food has to cross a courtyard – the kitchen is so far away for all I know it may have to cross a frontier. One toilet per floor...I just put my head round the door and wished I hadn't; no telephone that I could see and the beds so crammed together if you got out of one you'd be into another. Dreadful.

And of course I keep thinking of Ridgeways, the cup of tea, the matron's parlour and that immaculate lawn. It would break old Ralph's heart. But Ridgeways costs money. It always did. First of the month, beg to inform, respectfully submit, all very nice but £600 on the dot. And more. And more. And as Giles says, 'Mummy no can do. That kind of money we do not have.' Well we do, but it's all tied up.

And whereas in normal circumstances one would have fought tooth and nail to keep her in the private sector, just out of respect for Daddy, nowadays we are in what Giles calls a different ball game. And the old thing minds. Goodness, he minds. I wanted him to come with me today but just the idea of the place upsets him so much he won't even set foot in it. And actually I feel the same, but where is that going to get us? I thought of Ralph (as if I ever think of anybody else) and I thought, 'Come on, Muriel. You're a widow lady, you've got time on your hands, if anybody's in a position to roll their sleeves up it's you.' So today when I paid Mags a visit I got the name of the hospital secretary, almoner it used to be called in my day, and bearded him in his den. He did have a beard actually and looked pretty sorry for himself besides. It turns out he has to precept for absolutely everything down to the last toilet roll, and if he does have any brainwaves about improvements and can sell them to his own management committee, he's still at the mercy of the regional spending programme.

I asked about a table-tennis table. He said, 'My point exactly.' A table-tennis table would mean going cap in hand to Ipswich, which he's not anxious to do since the vegetable steamer's on its last legs. And on the rare occasions he does have a bit of latitude he finds his hands are tied by NUPE. Well, the upshot is I'm writing sheaves of letters to everybody I've ever heard of in an effort to plug the hospital into the coffee-morning circuit and get a support group started. What I'm saying is that mental illness is a scourge. It's also a mystery, can occur in the best-regulated families and nobody knows why. I mean, take us. Why have we been singled out? Loving parents. Perfectly normal childhood, then this.

When I went in this afternoon, Margaret was weaving a basket, and not making a bad stab at it really, all things considered. It's lucky I arrived when I did because she'd just got to the part where she had to integrate the handle with the main body and she was making a real pig's breakfast of it. So I got cracking and showed her the whys and wherefores and actually ended up making both handles. Which seemed to make her a lot happier. She's never been much good with her hands. Giles was a real wizard.

A propos Giles there's a bit of a crisis with the funds apparently. Nothing serious. A chum's let him down. Didn't read the small print. Says it's nothing to worry about, though we may have to pull our horns in a bit further. So I said, 'All hands to the pumps. With all Daddy's contacts in the City why don't I start up a little catering business, executive lunches and the like? Good nursery food and lashings of it.' Giles not sure. Thought these days they wanted something a bit more nouvelle. I laughed, I said, 'Don't you believe it. Men are overgrown schoolboys, always were. Preached salad at Ralph for years and what good did it do?' Giles said, 'Small detail, Mum: what are you going to use for capital?' So that put the tin hat on that one. It's this bloody liquidity thing. It's funny I never heard Ralph mention it.

GO TO BLACK.

Come up on Muriel in a bare unfurnished room. A suitcase open. A tea-chest. Afternoon.

Job sorting out the one or two things I want to keep, though quite honestly I'm not sorry to see the back of most of it. I feel it puts me more in the same boat as Ralph. Lay not up for yourself treasures on earth type thing. The lilies of the field syndrome. Said this to the vicar who was looking round. He thought this was a healthy attitude and how much did I think the walnut sidetable might fetch, it would go so well in their hall. Huge marquee on the lawn. People trooping through the house, and Angela Gillespie never away. Said how horrid it must be to see people poking about among one's prized possessions. I said, 'Yes,' but it isn't really. The person I do feel sorry for is Mabel, who's had it to polish all these years. Still, she was getting on like a house on fire with the auctioneer's men, who were all so careful and polite I'd have married any one of them on the spot. Angela beefing on about all the dealers being here, putting up the prices, I thought good job. Still, however much it all fetches it will only be a drop in the ocean.

At one point Angela got the Duttons in a corner and started telling the tale. Said Giles had always been a wrong 'un. I turned round and said she didn't know what she was talking about, it had been a genuine mistake. She said, 'Mistake? Hundreds of people losing their life savings a mistake?' I said, 'So why do you think I'm selling up?' She said, 'It wasn't your fault. Why should you suffer? That's what worries me, Muriel, it's not fair on you.' Fair on me or not it didn't stop her buying the corner cupboard. She's had her eye on it for years.

I suppose Giles has been a scamp. But I don't think he's been wicked. Just not very bright that's all. Still, Sloane Street is in Pippa's name so that's a blessing, and the school fees were covenanted for years ago so it's not all gloom. I sat under the chestnut tree while the sale was going on, and thought how none of this would have happened if Ralph hadn't died. Then I heard him say, 'Buck up, old girl,' and went and gave a hand with the tea. I haven't told Margaret yet. Her fourteen-year-old psychiatrist thinks this may not be the moment. Sees some signs of improvement. Margaret brought him some tulips last week. Picked them from one of the hospital flowerbeds. I apologised and said I could give them some of our bulbs. He said not at all, it was a sign she was becoming more outgoing. Wanted to know about Ralph and Margaret. I said, 'In what way?' He said, 'No particular way. When she was little.' I said, 'Ralph was fond of her: she was his little girl.' He said, 'Yes.'

Took the dogs up the hill later on. They're next I suppose. Bloody psychiatrist.

GO TO BLACK.

Come up on Muriel in a plain boarding-house room. Evening.

Crack of dawn this morning I routed out my trusty green cossy and spent a happy half-hour breasting the billows. The old cossy's seen better days and the moth has got into the bust but as the only people about were one or two brave souls walking the dog I didn't frighten the troops.

Came back hungry as a hunter so boiled myself an egg on the ring and had it with a slice of Ryvita, sitting in the window. Sun just catches it for an hour then, lovely. I tidied the room, did one or two jobs, and then toddled along to the library and had a walk round Boots by which time it was getting on for lunchtime, it's surprising how time does go. When I think of the things I used to get through in the old days I wonder how I did it.

Been here about a month now. Got onto it via an advert in *The Lady*. Sledmere it's called, 'Holiday flatlets'. Off season, of course, and quite reasonable. I haven't quite got the town sorted out yet. I feel sure there must be a community here if only I can put my finger on it. I had a word with a young woman at the Town Hall. Blue fingernails but civil enough otherwise. Said was I interested in Meals On Wheels. I said, 'Rather. I was 2 i/c Meals on Wheels for the whole of Sudbury,' a fund of experience. Brawn not too good but brains available to be picked at any time. She looked a bit blank. Turns out she meant did I want to be on the receiving end. I said, 'Not on your life.' But message received and understood. The old girl's past it. Hence the swim, I suppose.

Still, I soldier on and it's not quite orphans of the storm time. I look round the shops quite a bit and if I'm lucky I run into Angela Gillespie who's got her mother in a home here and comes over from time to time. We have coffee and a natter about the old days. Though I can't do that too often. Morning coffee these days seems to cost a king's ransom. And with me there doesn't have to be coffee. I can talk to anybody. The other morning I got chatting to one of these young men in orange who bang their tambourines in the precinct. Came up to me rattling his bowl, shaven head but otherwise quite sensible. His view is that life is some kind of prep. Trial run. Thinks we're being buffed up for a better role next time. As sensible as anything else I suppose. I said, 'Well, I just hope it's not in Hunstanton.' (*She laughs.*)

The big bright spot on the horizon is Margaret. Heaps better, lost a lot of weight, got rid of that terrible cardigan and now is quite a good-looking young woman. In a hostel up to pres. but planning on getting a small flat. Came down last week and says next time it could be under her own steam, takes her driving test in ten days. Miracle. She took me out to lunch just like a normal girl. Talked about Ralph etc. Doesn't blame him, wishes he were alive. I don't know what I think. Sorry for him, I suppose. She paid the bill and left a tip, just as if she'd been doing it all her life. Of course she'll be nicely off now, Ralph tied it all up so tight even Giles couldn't get his hands on it, the rascal.

Don't see him and Pippa much, not a peep out of them for over a month now. Doesn't like to come down, says it upsets him. Don't know why. Doesn't upset me. Miss the tinies. Not so tiny, Lucy'll be twelve now. And twelve is like fifteen. Married next. I'd seen myself as a model grandmother, taking them to *Peter Pan* and the Science Museum. Not to be. Another dream bites the dust.

My big passion now is the telly box. Never bothered with it before. These days I watch it all the time. And I'm not the discerning viewer. No fear. Rubbish. Australian series in the afternoons, everything. Glued to it all. Fan.

The dialogue is more broken up now.

I sometimes wonder if I killed Ralph. All those death-dealing breakfasts. We haven't had much weather to speak of. Eat less now. A buttered scone goes a long way.

She picks up a Walkman and headphones.

This is my new toy. Seen children with them, never appreciated what they were. Asked a young man for a listen in the precinct. Revelation. Saved up and bought one. Get the cassettes out of the library. Worth its weight in gold. Marvellous.

She puts it on and henceforth speaks in bursts and too loudly.

I wouldn't want you to think this was a tragic story.

Pause.

I'm not a tragic woman.

Pause.

I'm not that type.

FADE OUT *to the faint sound of the music, possibly Johann Strauss.*

A CREAM CRACKER UNDER THE SETTEE

Doris · Thora Hird
Policeman · Stephen Beard

DORIS IS IN HER SEVENTIES AND THE PLAY IS SET IN THE LIVING-ROOM AND HALLWAY OF HER SEMI-DETACHED HOUSE. SHE IS SITTING SLIGHTLY AWKWARDLY ON A LOW CHAIR AND RUBBING HER LEG. MORNING.

It's such a silly thing to have done.

Pause.

I should never have tried to dust. Zulema says to me every time she comes, 'Doris. Do not attempt to dust. The dusting is my department. That's what the council pay me for. You are now a lady of leisure. Your dusting days are over.' Which would be all right provided she did dust. But Zulema doesn't dust. She half-dusts. I know when a place isn't clean.

When she's going she says, 'Doris. I don't want to hear that you've been touching the Ewbank. The Ewbank is out of bounds.' I said, 'I could just run round with it now and again.' She said, 'You can't run anywhere. You're on trial here.' I said, 'What for?' She said, 'For being on your own. For not behaving sensibly. For not acting like a woman of seventy-five who has a pacemaker and dizzy spells and doesn't have the sense she was born with.' I said, 'Yes, Zulema.'

She says, 'What you don't understand, Doris, is that I am the only person that stands between you and Stafford House. I have to report on you. The Welfare say to me every time, "Well, Zulema, how is she coping? Wouldn't she be better off in Stafford House?"' I said, 'They don't put people in Stafford House just for running round with the Ewbank.' 'No,' she says. 'They bend over backwards to keep you in your own home. But, Doris, you've got to meet them halfway. You're seventy-five. Pull your horns in. You don't have to swill the flags. You don't have to clean the bath. Let the dirt wait. It won't kill you. I'm here every week.'

I was glad when she'd gone, dictating. I sat for a bit looking up at me and Wilfred on the wedding photo. And I thought, 'Well, Zulema, I bet you haven't dusted the top of that.' I used to be able to reach only I can't now. So I got the buffet and climbed up. And she hadn't. Thick with dust. Home help. Home hindrance. You're better off doing it yourself. And I was just wiping it over when, oh hell, the flaming buffet went over.

Pause.

You feel such a fool. I can just hear Zulema. 'Well, Doris, I did tell you.' Only I think I'm all right. My leg's a bit numb but I've managed to get back on the chair. I'm just going to sit and come round a bit. Shakes you up, a fall.

Pause.

Shan't let on I was dusting.

She shoves the duster down the side of the chair.

Dusting is forbidden.

She looks down at the wedding photo on the floor.

Cracked the photo. We're cracked, Wilfred.

Pause.

The gate's open again. I thought it had blown shut, only now it's blown open. Bang bang bang all morning, it'll be bang bang bang all afternoon.

Dogs coming in, all sorts. You see Zulema should have closed that, only she didn't.

Pause.

The sneck's loose, that's the root cause of it. It's wanted doing for years. I kept saying to Wilfred, 'When are you going to get round to that gate?' But oh no. It was always the same refrain. 'Don't worry, Mother. I've got it on my list.' I never saw no list. He had no list. I was the one with the list. He'd no system at all, Wilfred. 'When I get a minute, Doris.' Well, he's got a minute now, bless him.

Pause.

Feels funny this leg. Not there.

Pause

Some leaves coming down now. I could do with trees if they didn't have leaves, going up and down the path. Zulema won't touch them. Says if I want leaves swept I've to contact the Parks Department.

I wouldn't care if they were my leaves. They're not my leaves. They're next-door's leaves. We don't have any leaves. I know that for a fact. We've only got the one little bush and it's an evergreen, so I'm certain they're not my leaves. Only other folks won't know that. They see the bush and they see the path and they think, 'Them's her leaves.' Well, they're not.

I ought to put a note on the gate. 'Not my leaves.' Not my leg either, the way it feels. Gone to sleep.

Pause.

I didn't even want the bush, to be quite honest. We debated it for long enough. I said, 'Dad. Is it a bush that will make a mess?' He said, 'Doris. Rest assured. This type of bush is very easy to follow,' and fetches out the catalogue. '"This labour-saving variety is much favoured by retired people." Anyway,' he says, 'the garden is my department.' Garden! It's only the size of a tablecloth. I said, 'Given a choice, Wilfred, I'd have preferred concrete.' He said, 'Doris. Concrete has no character.' I said, 'Never mind character, Wilfred, where does hygiene come on the agenda?' With concrete you can feel easy in your mind. But no. He had to have his little garden even if it was only a bush. Well, he's got his little garden now. Only I bet that's covered in leaves. Graves, gardens, everything's to follow.

I'll make a move in a minute. See if I can't put the kettle on. Come on leg. Wake up.

GO TO BLACK.

Come up on Doris sitting on the floor with her back to the wall. The edge of a tiled fireplace also in shot.

Fancy, there's a cream cracker under the settee. How long has that been there? I can't think when I last had cream crackers.

She's not half done this place, Zulema.

I'm going to save that cream cracker and show it her next time she starts going on about Stafford House. I'll say, 'Don't Stafford House me, lady. This cream cracker was under the settee. I've only got to send this cream cracker to the Director of Social Services and you'll be on the carpet. Same as the cream cracker. I'll be in Stafford House, Zulema, but you'll be in the Unemployment Exchange.'

I'm en route for the window only I'm not making much headway. I'll bang on it. Alert somebody. Don't know who. Don't know anybody round here now. Folks opposite, I don't know them. Used to be the Marsdens. Mr and Mrs Marsden and Yvonne, the funny daughter. There for years. Here before we were, the Marsdens. Then he died, and she died, and Yvonne went away somewhere. A home, I expect.

Smartish woman after them. Worked at Wheatley and Whiteley, had a three-quarter-length coat. Used to fetch the envelopes round for the blind. Then she went and folks started to come and go. You lose track. I don't think they're married, half of them. You see all sorts. They come in the garden and behave like animals. I find the evidence in a morning.

She picks up the photograph that has fallen from the wall.

Now, Wilfred.

Pause.

I can nip this leg and nothing.

Pause.

Ought to have had a dog. Then it could have been barking of someone. Wilfred was always hankering after a dog. I wasn't keen. Hairs all up and down, then having to take it outside every five minutes. Wilfred said he would be prepared to undertake that responsibility. The dog would be his province. I said, 'Yes, and whose province would all the little hairs be?' I gave in in the finish, only I said it had to be on the small side. I didn't want one of them great lolloping, lamppost-smelling articles. And we never got one either. It was the growing mushrooms in the cellar saga all over again. He never got round to it. A kiddy'd've solved all that. Getting mad ideas. Like the fretwork, making toys and forts and whatnot. No end of money he was going to make. Then there was his phantom allotment. Oh, he was going to be coming home with leeks and spring cabbage and I don't know what. 'We can be self-sufficient in the vegetable department, Doris.' Never materialised. I was glad. It'd've meant muck somehow.

Hello. Somebody coming. Salvation.

She cranes up towards the window.

Young lad. Hello. Hello.

She begins to wave.

The cheeky monkey. He's spending a penny. Hey.

She shouts.

Hey. Get out. Go on. Clear off. You little demon. Would you credit it? Inside our gate. Broad daylight. The place'll stink.

A pause as she realises what she has done.

He wouldn't have known what to do anyway. Only a kiddy. The policeman comes past now and again. If I can catch him. Maybe the door's a better bet. If I can get there I can open it and wait while somebody comes past.

She starts to heave herself up.

This must be what they give them them frame things for.

GO TO BLACK.

Come up on Doris sitting on the floor in the hall, her back against the front door, the letter-box above her head.

This is where we had the pram. You couldn't get past for it. Proper prams then, springs and hoods. Big wheels. More like cars than prams. Not these fold-up jobs. You were proud of your pram. Wilfred spotted it in the *Evening Post*. I said, 'Don't let's jump the gun, Wilfred.' He said, 'At that price, Doris? This is the chance of a lifetime.'

Pause.

Comes under this door like a knife. I can't reach the lock. That's part of the Zulema regime. 'Lock it and put it on the chain, Doris. You never know who comes. It may not be a bona fide caller.' It never is a bona fide caller. I never get a bona fide caller.

Couple came round last week. Braying on the door. They weren't bona fide callers, they had a Bible. I didn't go. Only they opened the letter-box and started shouting about Jesus. 'Good news,' they kept shouting. 'Good news.' They left the gate open, never mind good news. They ought to get their priorities right. They want learning that on their instruction course. Shouting about Jesus and leaving gates open. It's hypocrisy is that. It is in my book anyway. 'Love God and close all gates.'

She closes her eyes. We hear some swift steps up the path and the letter-box opens as a leaflet comes through. Swift steps away again as she opens her eyes.

Hello, hello.

She bangs on the door behind her.

Help. Help. Oh stink.

She tries to reach the leaflet.

What is it? Minicabs? 'Your roof repaired'?

She gets the leaflet.

'Grand carpet sale.' Carpet sales in chapels now. Else Sikhs.

She looks at the place where the pram was.

I wanted him called John. The midwife said he wasn't fit to be called anything and had we any newspaper? Wilfred said, 'Oh yes. She saves newspaper. She saves shoeboxes as well.' I must have fallen asleep because when I woke up she'd gone. I wanted to see to him. Wrapping him in newspaper as if he was dirty. He wasn't dirty, little thing. I don't think Wilfred minded. A kiddy. It was the same as the allotment and the fretwork. Just a craze. He said, 'We're better off, Doris. Just the two of us.' It was then he started talking about getting a dog.

If it had lived I might have had grandchildren now. Wouldn't have been in this fix. Daughters are best. They don't migrate.

Pause.

I'm going to have to migrate or I'll catch my death.

She nips her other leg.

This one's going numb now.

She picks up the photo.

Come on, Dad. Come on, numby leg.

GO TO BLACK.

Come up on Doris sitting with her back against the settee under which she spotted the cream cracker. It is getting dark.

I've had this frock for years. A lame woman ran it up for me that lived down Tong Road. She made me a little jersey costume I used to wear with my tan court shoes. I think I've still got it somewhere. Upstairs. Put away. I've got umpteen pillowcases, some we got given when we were first married. Never used. And the blanket I knitted for the cot. All its little coats and hats.

She puts her hand down.

Here's this cream cracker.

She rubs it.

Naught wrong with it.

She eats it.

Making a lot of crumbs. Have to have a surreptitious go with the Ewbank. 'Doris. The Ewbank is out of bounds.' Out of bounds to her too, by the looks of it. A cream cracker under the settee. She wants reporting. Can't report her now. I've destroyed the evidence.

Pause.

I could put another one under, they'd never know. Except they might say it was me. 'Squatting biscuits under the settee, Doris. You're not fit to be on your own. You'd be better off in Stafford House.'

Pause.

We were always on our own, me and Wilfred. We weren't gregarious. We just weren't the gregarious type. He thought he was, but he wasn't.

Mix. I don't want to mix. Comes to the finish and they suddenly think you want to mix. I don't want to be stuck with a lot of old lasses. And they all smell of pee. And daft half of them, banging tambourines. You go daft there, there's nowhere else for you to go but daft. Wearing somebody else's frock. They even mix up your teeth. I am H.A.P.P.Y. I am not H.A.P.P.Y. I am un-H.A.P.P.Y. Or I would be.

And Zulema says, 'You don't understand, Doris. You're not up to date. They have lockers, now. Flowerbeds. They have their hair done. They go on trips to Wharfedale.' I said, 'Yes. Smelling of pee.' She said, 'You're prejudiced, you.' I said, 'I am, where hygiene's concerned.'

When people were clean and the streets were clean and it was all clean and you could walk down the street and folks smiled and passed the time of day, I'd leave the door on the latch and go on to the end for some toffee, and when I came back Dad was home and the cloth was on and the plates out and we'd have our tea. Then we'd side the pots and I'd wash up while he read the paper and we'd eat the toffees and listen to the wireless all them years ago when we were first married and I was having the baby.

Doris and Wilfred. They don't get called Doris now. They don't get called Wilfred. Museum, names like that. That's what they're all called in Stafford House. Alice and Doris. Mabel and Gladys. Antiques. Keep them under lock and key. 'What's your name? Doris? Right. Pack your case. You belong in Stafford House.'

A home. Not me. No fear.

She closes her eyes. A pause.

POLICEMAN'S VOICE. Hello. Hello.

Doris opens her eyes but doesn't speak.

Are you all right?

Pause.

DORIS. No. I'm all right.

POLICEMAN. Are you sure?

DORIS. Yes.

POLICEMAN. Your light was off.

DORIS. I was having a nap.

POLICEMAN. Sorry. Take care.

He goes.

DORIS. Thank you.

She calls again.

Thank you.

Long pause.

You've done it now, Doris. Done it now, Wilfred.

Pause.

I wish I was ready for bed. All washed and in a clean nightie and the bottle in, all sweet and crisp and clean like when I was little on Baking Night, sat in front of the fire with my long hair still.

Her eyes close and she sings a little to herself. The song, which she only half remembers, is My Alice Blue Gown.

Pause.

Never mind. It's done with now, anyway.

LIGHT FADES.

INTRODUCTION TO TALKING HEADS 2

These six monologues have been a long time coming: I've been intermittently trying to write them since 1988 when the first series went out. Had I not stopped at six then, I think I could have gone on and written another half dozen without too much trouble, but seeing the first lot produced with a measure of success made the next batch harder to do. I've kept putting them aside and even when they were, in effect, finished I left them in a drawer for a year as I felt they were too gloomy to visit on the public.

This gloom is not deliberate: it is just the way they have turned out. Nor is it that, as I grow older, I take a grimmer view of the world. It's simply that, though I may sit down with the intention of writing something funny, it seldom comes out that way any more. I don't feel called upon to offer any further explanation, though I shall doubtless be asked to account for it, if only by students.

A few years after the televising of the first series of *Talking Heads* they were made part of the A Level syllabus. While I was not unflattered by this it did land me with dozens of letters from candidates wanting a low-down on the text. Some of them, it was plain, thought that writing to the author was a useful way of getting their homework done for them; others were more serious, genuinely feeling that I could give them some clues as to the inner meaning of what I had written. I fell in with very few of these requests, generally sending a postcard saying that their ideas about the monologues were as good as mine and they should treat me like a dead author, who was thus unavailable for comment.

This was not entirely facetious. A playwright is not the best person to talk about his own work for the simple reason that he is often unaware of what he has written. Someone (I think, Tom Stoppard) has compared the playwright confronted by his critics to a passage through Customs. Under the impression he has nothing to declare the playwright heads confidently for the Green exit. Alerted (and irritated) by this air of confidence an official of the Customs and Excise steps forward and asks our writer formally 'Have you any contraband?' 'No,' smiles the playwright. 'Very well,' says the officer, 'kindly open your suitcase.' Happy to comply (he has nothing to be ashamed of, after all) the playwright throws back the lid. Whereupon to his horror there lie revealed a pair of disgustingly dirty underpants and some extremely pungent socks. The playwright is covered in confusion; for though these underpants are undoubtedly his and the socks too, nevertheless he has no recollection of having packed them, still less of giving them pride of place on top of his belongings. The customs officer sniffs (as well he might). However, since there is as yet no law against the import of dirty underpants or smelly socks, the officer gingerly puts them on one side and delves further into the playwright's case.

The next revelation is some photographs. These too take the playwright by surprise. Had he packed them? Surely not. But they are most certainly his: this is a photograph of his father and here are three photographs of his mother and at least half a dozen of himself. 'Rather fond of ourselves, aren't we sir?' murmurs the customs man insolently. The playwright stammers some excuse, only thankful that the snaps are after all quite decent. But his relief is premature because, after sifting through yet more soiled clothing, the customs man now unearths another photograph: it is the playwright again, only this time he has his trousers down, he is smiling and with every appearance of pride he is showing his bottom to the camera. Now not only does the playwright not remember packing this photograph, he doesn't even remember it being taken. But this is him; those are his trousers; that is his smile and, yes, that, without question, is his bottom. 'One of our holiday snaps is it, sir?' sneers the customs officer. 'I should keep that covered up if I were you. We all have one, you know.'

And so the embarrassing examination goes on, the searcher uncovering ever more outrageous items – ideas the playwright thought he had long since discarded, an old marriage, a dead teacher and even a body or two locked in a long forgotten embrace, none of which the playwright ever dreamed of packing but which somehow have found their way into this commodious suitcase, his play.

So there is not much point in my telling you or the A Level students what *Talking Heads* is about or what I have put into my particular suitcase. All I can do is list some of the contents, note some of the themes (or at any rate recurrences), trace the origins of some of these pieces (insofar as I am aware of them) and link them occasionally with other stuff that I've written, always remembering that the relationship between life and art is never as straightforward as the reader or the audience tend to imagine.

That fictional characters are not drawn directly from life is a truism. Evelyn Waugh's epigraph to *Brideshead Revisited* puts it succinctly: 'I am not I; thou are not he or she; they are not they.' But such a straightforward disavowal is misleading, because characters are taken from life: it's just that they are seldom yanked out of it quite so unceremoniously as the public imagines. They aren't hi-jacked unchanged into art or shoved just as they are onto the page or in front of the camera: the playwright or novelist has to take them to Costume or Make-up in order to alter their appearance and sometimes he even takes them to a surgeon to change their sex. So that when the writer has finished with them they come on as someone far removed from the character they started off as, yet still, as in dreams, sharing his or her original identity.

And as it is with characters so it is with places. I hope no one ever tries to construct an exact topography of these or any of my other plays because I use street names at random, generally picking out the names I remember from my childhood in Leeds regardless of their geographical location. The posh suburbs then were Lawnswood and Alwoodley, and that still holds good, but otherwise the place I have in my head is only distantly related to Leeds as it is now and as in dreams, again, one landscape adjoins another without logic or possibility. In *Playing Sandwiches*, for instance, Wilfred has been an attendant at the Derby Baths, but of course the Derby Baths aren't in Leeds, they're in Blackpool, as I'm sure many viewers will write and tell me. I imagine that in my cavalier (or slipshod) attitude to topography I'm not untypical which leads me to suppose that handbooks to Proust, say, or keys to Dickens, tell only a fraction of the truth.

I note the recurrences, which may indicate preoccupations, though they may equally well betray the poverty of my imagination: there are two dogs, for instance, one a chow with an arthritic hip that gets to run along the Scarborough sands in *Miss Fozzard Finds Her Feet*, the other a noisy alsatian which gets its owner acquitted in *The Outside Dog*. It was only when the monologues were being edited that I realised I had called both dogs Tina, which in *A Woman of No Importance* is also the name of Mr Cressell and Mr Rudyard's Jack Russell.

Two characters have strokes; two receive counselling; one husband is a murderer, another character is said to be a murderer (by virtue of being a tobacconist); and another husband gets murdered. The murders mystify me, the strokes less so as I am getting to the age when that sort of thing begins to nag, though that isn't really why they figure here. What can or cannot be said is a staple of the drama and it's in this regard rather than attempting an accurate depiction of the condition that I've written about strokes. Or 'cerebral incidents' as neurologists tend to call them nowadays, doctors as inhibited in their own speech as some of the stricken patients whom they are treating.

That Violet's account of the last visit of her sweetheart should be flawless is perhaps a romanticised view of aphasia, owing something to the occasional dispensation from their symptoms enjoyed by Parkinsonian patients rather than stroke victims. Violet's remark that if she could sing everything then she wouldn't forget, is more true of sufferers from Parkinson's than it is of those incapacitated by a stroke, Parkinsonians sometimes being able to dance through a door when they are incapable of walking through it.

The press are several times unkindly noticed though not, I think, unfairly. Having on several occasions had to put up with their intrusions myself, I find I now make no distinction between reporters from the *Daily Mail* or journalists from the *Guardian*: they are more like each other than they are ordinary human beings.

Though neither the *Mail* nor the *Guardian* is a Murdoch paper, Murdoch is certainly to blame for pushing down standards not merely, as Dennis Potter said in his final interview, in journalism but in politics too and other areas of the nation's life. The danger with Mr Murdoch is that he has been around now for long enough to have mellowed into a familiar villain whose unscrupulous behaviour no longer surprises; because he is so routinely self-seeking we have begun to take it with a shrug if not a smile. So it would have been with Hitler had he lived, *Desert Island Discs* the English reward for a long life, however ill-spent.

I note the absence of children. Nearly all these women are childless, only ninety-five-year-old Violet having a son but whom she doesn't recognise as such because, with his 'big wristwatch, attaché case and one of those green raincoaty-things they shoot in', he looks more like a father than a son. No one else has children, not even in Australia where I've sometimes posted inconvenient offspring much as they did in the nineteenth century. I suppose I feel that children blur the picture and mitigate the sadness and, bringing their own problems with them, they demand to be attended to, and want to put their spoke in and are every bit as awkward in the drama as they are in life but with none of the compensations. One thing at a time is my motto and keep children out of it.

There's no sense in Wilfred having a child in *Playing Sandwiches* because the audience would just be waiting for him to interfere with it. Miss Fozzard is unmarried and past child-bearing anyway: I suspect, though, she wouldn't care for children particularly in the context of soft furnishings. Nor would Celia, the owner of the antique shop in *The Hand of God*. With her philosophy of,

> 'Lovely to look at, nice to hold,
> but if you break it
> I say Sold!'

she wouldn't want small hands picking up her bibelots. I was once in an antique shop which a (not very unruly) child had just left. 'No,' said the woman behind the counter, 'I don't care for children, and that was a particularly bad example of the genre.'

On the other hand a child might have helped both Marjory in *The Outside Dog* and Rosemary in *Nights in the Gardens of Spain*, taking Marjory's mind off housework and Rosemary's off the garden. But it would also have meant there would have been no story to tell.

Another omission is, of course, the television set, which one would expect to be chattering away in the corner of many of these rooms but which must invariably be censored by playwrights protective of their dialogue. These are not naturalistic pieces but even plays that claim to be faithful accounts of ordinary life can seldom accommodate this garrulous intruder. The world of everything that is the case is not the world of drama.

Miss Fozzard Finds Her Feet is my second stab at chiropody, the first being *A Private Function* in 1985. I have no idea why chiropodists should strike such a chord, though when my mother was getting on and I had to sit in on a visit by the local chiropodist the situation did feel quite comic. Bernard's reference to 'your foot feller' is taken from another visit by the same chiropodist: finding my parents out, he left the time of their appointment with a neighbour, who, unable to spell chiropodist, put a note through the door saying, 'Foot Feller, Tuesday

3.30'. Finding the note my father claimed he thought it was a racing tip.

Feet did figure in my childhood as one of my aunties worked in Manfield's shoe shop on Commercial Street in Leeds and when she came round to see us in the evening she would regale us with all the events of her day, told in Proustian detail. When the door eventually closed behind her Dad would burst out, 'I wouldn't care but you're no further on when she's done.'

The names of shoes, the 'fur-lined Gibson bruised look' which Mr Dunderdale has Miss Fozzard try on, comes from twenty years ago when I was filming in an old-fashioned shoe shop in West Hartlepool. Feeling this was what proper writers did I took down a selection of names of shoes from the boxes stacked on the high shelves. I am sure the ankle-hugging bootee in Bengal bronze that Mr Dunderdale gives to Miss Fozzard is not a 'fur-lined Gibson bruised look' and I suppose I could verify this by walking down the road to Camden High Street where, to the detriment of the street as a decent shopping centre, every other shop is a shoe shop. But perhaps not, the expertise of the assistants in Camden stretching to the knowledge that shoes go on the feet but not much beyond that.

The department store where Miss Fozzard presides over Soft Furnishings is called Matthias Robinson's, which was indeed a department store on Briggate in Leeds and which closed early in the sixties. The name itself is sufficient to stamp it as an old-fashioned emporium of which there were many in Leeds: Wheatley and Whiteley, Marsh Jones and Cribb, Marshall and Snelgrove and in Bradford, memorably, Brown Muff's. Marshall and Snelgrove was a smarter store than Matthias Robinson's but both had the same hushed, carpeted elegance, soft lighting and snooty assistants (like Miss Fozzard) who called my mother 'madam' and so got her all flustered. Near where Matthias Robinson's stood is now Harvey Nichols which aspires, I suppose, to be the smartest store in Leeds though nowhere quite captures the elegance of those grander stores or their seductive smell, a blend of perfume, leather, warm carpet and (in Bradford particularly) fur coats.

When the Sistine Chapel was being restored in the 1980s, anyone with influence in the art world would be taken up in the lift to watch the restorers at work. Thus it was that several people I came across claimed to have reached out and touched either the hand of God or the finger of Adam. Easy-going as the Italians are I would be surprised if these accounts were altogether true but they gave me the idea for the beginning of a film script, *The Hand of God*, which I wrote but never managed to get produced. The script centred round a priceless drawing by Michelangelo of the hand of God wearing the ring of Michelangelo's patron, Julius II, and it's this drawing which (never having made it into a film script) turns up in the box of odds and ends grudgingly given to Celia on the death of Miss Ventriss.

'If you love beautiful things,' says Celia, 'which is why I came into this business in the first place, it breaks your heart.' I detect here a thirty-year-old echo of the only TV comedy series I ever did, *On the Margin*. The first programme featured an antique shop, with myself as the camp proprietor:

> DEALER. If you don't see what you want you've only got to ask. I don't put everything in the shop window.
>
> CUSTOMER. Could I just sort of nose around?
>
> DEALER. Feel free. You must excuse my hands but I've just been stripping a tallboy.
>
> [All this seemed quite daring in 1966.]

> Mind you I'm not in this business to make money. I'm in this business because I like beautiful things and I like beautiful people to have beautiful things. Which is why I'm very anxious to sell something to you. You see, I believe, perhaps wrongly, that if only all the beautiful people in the world had all the beautiful things there would be No More War. Don't you agree?

There is some irony in the fact that this blueprint for world peace was addressed to the young John Sergeant, who played the Customer but who is now the doyen of the BBC's political correspondents.

Nowadays antique shops are getting thin on the ground, most selling done not through shops but at antique fairs and car boot sales. It's an altogether more knowing business than it was, Sotheby's and Christie's having started the process and shaken down the country in quest of anything saleable. Celia remarks that Sotheby's and Christie's are no better than barrow boys: rather worse, in my view, as barrow boys don't charge a percentage to both buyer and seller and make them feel socially inferior into the bargain. Then there's the *Antiques Road Show* which has set everyone scouring their attics and fetching out their cherished heirlooms. Despite their eagerness to know the value of their precious possessions I have never seen anyone on the programme admit to wanting to sell the objects in question. It's a cosy contribution to our national hypocrisy.

I imagine Celia's shop as bare and uninviting, full of big furniture with not much in it in the way of bric-a-brac, the kind of shop I'd think twice about going into. Such establishments, though, are no longer the norm. Antique shops, as Celia would be the first to point out, have come down in the world. Typical stock nowadays might be a lace doyley; a napkin ring; a Penguin Special from the forties; an empty scent spray from a thirties' dressing table, redolent of long-dead 4711, and an old Oxo tin. Not antiques at all, of course, but 'collectables'.

And collectables that tread hard on the heels of the present so one is nowadays regularly confronted by items classified as antiques which one remembers in common use. Milk was brought round from door to door when I was a boy by Mr Keen the milkman with his horse and cart – and this in suburban Armley. The milk was ladled out of his lidded oval pail in gill measures, both pail and measure now regularly on offer in antique shops, the pewter buffed, the brass polished and both, I suppose, serving ultimately as receptacles for flowers or the ubiquitous pot-pourri. The history of popular taste in the eighties and nineties could be charted via the march of pot-pourri; in the twenties scenting Ottoline Morrell's lacquered rooms at Garsington, today, as Celia points out, on sale at any garage.

I miss the old-fashioned antique shops: Slee's on the upper floors of premises on Boar Lane in Leeds, where the stock was so shabby and slow-moving it seemed as if it had been aged on the premises; Taylor's in Harrogate which had in its window photographs of that famous magpie, Queen Mary, emerging from the shop in her toque and parasol, with some hapless lady-in-waiting bringing up the rear with the articles Her Majesty had admired and which etiquette demanded she must forthwith be given. Another classy establishment was Frank Williams' in Burford in Oxfordshire where I remember first going forty years ago as an undergraduate and which is now reduced to selling shirts, though at least it doesn't sell the 'pictures of mice in pinnies-type-thing' that Celia groans about (though there's no shortage of that in Burford either). And I know all this is snobbish and strikes the *lacrimae rerum* note; I should leave Celia, though a far from sympathetic character, to voice my regrets and reminiscences for me.

I realise, incidentally, as I write that the finger of God which is Celia's downfall is (and it was entirely unintentional) the finger that singles out the winners of the National Lottery.

Just as in the first series of *Talking Heads* there is only one male monologue and five by women. After that series a viewer wrote to me suggesting that if I wrote a series wholly for men I could call it *Talking Balls*. Which, had I been able to write six male monologues, I would happily have done. That I can't, I put down to the fact that when I was a child the women did most of the talking so that I've been more attuned to the discourse of women than to that of men, and though such real life monologues I come across nowadays are generally in the mouths of men I don't find male talk easy to reproduce; though it's easier when the men are damaged as Wilfred is in *Playing Sandwiches* and Graham in *A Chip in the Sugar*.

Playing Sandwiches dates back twenty years and is linked to a very different play, *The Old Country*, in which the main character, Hilary, is, or has been, a Soviet spy working in the Foreign Office. Accustomed to rendezvous with his Russian opposite number at various locations in London's outer suburbs he recalls how by sheer chance he nearly came to grief:

> It's quite hard to be absolutely alone. I never have. Though I have seen it. One particular afternoon I had been on one of my little jaunts, kept my appointment. Nothing unusual had occurred or was in the least likely to occur. It was a routine Thursday and I strolled back

to the station across a piece of waste ground that I knew made a nice short cut. I must have seemed a slightly incongruous figure in my city clothes. I never dressed the part, even to the extent of an old raincoat. At which point I came over the brow of the hill and found myself facing a line of policemen, advancing slowly through the undergrowth, poking in ditches with long sticks, hunting for something. It appeared there was a child missing, believed dead. Clothes had been found; a shoe. It was a bad moment. I had no reason at all for being there. I was a senior official in the Foreign Office. What was I doing on a spring afternoon, with documents in my briefcase, crossing a common where a child had been murdered? As it was no one thought to ask me any questions at all. I looked too respectable. And indeed they already had a suspect waiting handcuffed in the police car. I joined in the search and was with them when they found the child about half an hour later, lying in a heap at the foot of a wall. I just got a glimpse of her legs, white, like mushrooms, before they threw a blanket over her. She had been dead a week. I saw the man as the police car drew away through lines of jeering housewives and people cycling home from work. Then they threw a blanket over him too. The handy blanket. And I have a feeling he was eventually hanged. Anyway it was in those days. I came back, replaced the documents, had my tea by the fire in the Foreign Office. I took in some parliamentary questions for the minister, had dinner at the Garrick and walked home across the park. And in a tiled room at Uxbridge Police Station there would have been that

> young man waiting. Alone in a cell. Alone in custody. Alone at large. A man without home or haven. That is what you have to do to be cast out. Murder children. Nothing else quite does the trick, because any other crime will always find you friends. Rape them, kill them and be caught.
> (*The Old Country*, pp. 52–3)

The young man has had to wait twenty years for his case to be considered so he is no longer quite so young or living in the metropolitan suburbs but two hundred miles north near a municipal park. But it is the same man.

I am repelled by the self-righteous morality of gaols and their hierarchy of offences whereby murder and grievous bodily harm are thought of as respectable crimes and sexual offences are not. I also feel that the press hysteria over paedophilia, and in particular over offences that occurred long in the past, has reached dangerous proportions and the availability of monetary compensation for the possible psychological effects of these injuries has made the situation more fraught with difficulties. But such is the atmosphere surrounding the subject that one thinks twice before setting out any opinions one might have on the matter.

Murder is a messy business and for Marjory in *The Outside Dog* one feels it's just another skirmish in her continuing campaign against dirt. Even a more balanced character like Rosemary in *Nights in the Gardens of Spain* shares some of the same concerns so her first thought in seeing Mr McCorquodale's blood on the sheepskin rug is what a job it's going to be getting it off.

Somewhere Proust says that no matter how sad the occasion with women it will eventually resolve itself into a question of trying on. It could, more charitably, be said to turn into a question of cleaning down, though that's a side of life Proust didn't see much of.

Keeping dirt at bay in the way that Marjory does used to take up a substantial part of every housewife's day: there was the shaking of the rugs, the blackleading of the range, having a run round with the Ewbank, not to mention putting mountains of washing through the wringer. This was the lot of every self-respecting housewife in Leeds in my childhood, where in addition to the soot there was a continuous rain of fine grit from Kirkstall Power Station.

For a woman to adhere to such a routine (and the assumptions behind it) today seems wilful or neurotic, a deliberate narrowing of the scope and satisfactions of her sex. In those days keeping a clean house was the be-all and end-all, every day the occasion for the ceremony of purification, the successive stages of which culminated around the middle of the afternoon with the celebrant sinking into a chair before making the solemn declaration, 'This is the first time I've sat down all day.' There would then be a brief interval before the children came home from school and the men from work and the place was turned upside down again.

I see my mother sitting by the newly blackleaded range, her leg nearest the grate mottled blue-black by the fire as women's legs often were then, and saying imploringly, 'I've just got the place straight. Don't upset.'

This is not the first time I have written about it:

1 May 1978, Hartlepool (*Afternoon Off*)

We film in the sluice room of the cottage hospital. Racks of stainless-steel bottles and bedpans, a sink that flushes and a hideously stained drum on which the bedpans are sluiced out. This room would be my mother's nightmare. Conditions are cramped and I crouch behind the camera tripod in order to see the action. I am kneeling on the floor under the bedpan sluice. If my Mam saw this she would want to throw away trousers, raincoat, every particle of clothing that might have been touched and polluted. This has got into the film. Thora Hird plays a patient in the hospital being visited by her husband.

> 'I bet the house is upside down,' she says to him.
> 'It never is,' says her husband. 'I did the kitchen floor this morning.'
> 'Which bucket did you use?'
> 'The red one.'
> She is outraged. 'That's the outside bucket. I shall have it all to do again.

I am assuming this is common ground and that the tortuous boundary between the clean and the dirty is a frontier most households share. It was very marked in ours. My mother maintained an intricate hierarchy of cloths, buckets and dusters, to the Byzantine differentiations of which she alone was privy. Some cloths were dish cloths but not sink cloths; some were for the sink but not for the floor. There were dirty buckets and clean buckets, brushes for indoors, brushes for the flags. One mop had a universal application while another had a unique and terrible purpose and had to be kept outside, hung on the wall. And however rinsed and clean these utensils were they remained tainted by their awful

> function. Left to himself my Dad would violate these taboos, using the first thing that came to hand to clean the hearth or wash the floor. 'It's all nowt,' he'd mutter, but if Mam was around he knew it saved time and temper to observe her order of things. Latterly, disposable cloths and kitchen rolls tended to blur these ancient distinctions but the basic structure remained, perhaps the firmest part of the framework of her world. When she was ill with depression the order broke down: the house became dirty. Spotless though Dad kept it, she saw it as 'upside down', dust an unstemmable tide and the house's (imagined) squalor a talking point for the neighbours. So that when she came home from the hospital, bright and better, her first comment was always how clean the house looked. And not merely the house. It was as if the whole world and her existence in it had been rinsed clean.
> (*Writing Home*, pp. 277–8)

As a child I had a recurring dream, imperfectly dramatised in my play *Intensive Care*, in which my mother and I were sitting in a spotless house when suddenly the coalman burst through the door and trailed muck throughout the house. Though the dream owed something to the then adverts for Walpamur in which a child covered an immaculate wall with dirty hand prints, looking back I see that this intrusive coalman was probably my father, which accounts for the fact that, despite my alarm, my mother took this intrusion quite calmly. I can see that *The Outside Dog* is another version of this dream; not that that is much help to the viewer or the reader, though it may be useful fodder for the A Level candidates.

The Vale of York, where the open prison is located in *Nights in the Gardens of Spain* and where Rosemary and Mrs McCorquodale go on some of their jaunts, was just out of biking range when I was a boy and so seldom visited. Pre-prairified and dotted with ancient villages, duck ponds and grand country houses, it was a distant sunlit idyll and seemed to me a foretaste of what life must be like Down South. It was England as it was written about in children's books, and because I go there seldom still, it has retained some of this enchantment. Visiting country churches, which I used to do as a boy, is something I've rediscovered in middle age so in that sense I identify with Rosemary though not where gardening is concerned. I am no gardener, never managing to take a long enough view of things, finding the whole business not unstressful; I see the battle against weeds (ground elder in particular) as a fight against evil and one which invariably puts me in a bad temper.

Prison for Mrs McCorquodale is a kind of release just as it was for Miss Ruddock in *A Lady of Letters* in the first *Talking Heads*. This is a romanticised view, I'm sure, and having occasionally had to speak in men's prisons it is not a view I would so glibly advance on their behalf. I tend to regard women's prisons as women's institutes with bars on the windows, a prison sentence an ideal opportunity to brush up on the rug-making or learn French. If it were ever so it is not so now, education and vocational training in both men's and women's prisons the first victims of cut-backs.

I was put off writing *Waiting for the Telegram* for a long time because of the purely practical consideration that Violet would have to be impossibly old (nearly a hundred) to have had a sweetheart killed in the First War. And, of course, the longer I delayed writing the script the more acute the problem became. Eventually I decided that the time factor didn't really matter: in an old people's home time goes at a trickle anyway, what year it is is not of much consequence, least of all to the residents whose own age is often something of a mystery as it certainly is to Violet.

I see her living as a girl up Tong Road in Leeds, the route traversed by the No. 16 tram, the tram Violet feels she should have told Spencer about. It was a neighbourhood close-packed with red brick back-to-backs, including 'The Avenues', a run of eighteen streets named by their number, First Avenue, Second Avenue and so on. This was instanced in some sociological account I read as an example of the soullessness of nineteenth-century slum development but it wasn't quite like that. Each avenue had an atmosphere of its own, some certainly better (more genteel), others rougher or dirtier but far from being components in a featureless urban desert that the bare numbers might suggest.

Tong Road, with Sleights the greengrocers, Burras Peake's the outfitters, Gallons the grocers, and Hustwitt's the sheet music and gramophone shop, has long since gone – all that is left the unchanging black silhouette of St Bartholomew's and, a few streets over, Armley Gaol, twin bulwarks of church and state. Nowadays, with flimsy new houses clustered around the gaol, Tong Road seems bleaker than it ever was and certainly with less character, though doubtless a child brought up there today would be able to discriminate between its seemingly identical streets as effortlessly as we did then.

Some question arose during the rehearsing of the piece about the nature of a vanilla slice. It is, I suppose, a down-market version of a millefeuille, with confectioner's custard sandwiched between layers of flaky pastry and topped off with white icing. Someone bringing vanilla slices home from the confectioner's, fancies too, and certainly fruit pies, would bear the bag like the priest the host, held high on the flat of the hand lest the fruit leak out or the icing adhere to the paper bag. It's a sight – a rite almost – that I associate with Saturday dinner-time when we would be sent 'on to the end' to McDade's, the confectioner's on the corner of Tong Road and Gilpin Place, to get something 'to finish off with'.

Violet keeps being told she will soon be getting a telegram from the Queen, though whether that custom persists and whether it is a telegram I am not sure, though doubtless I shall be told. Telegraph boys still rode the streets on their high bicycles when I was a boy, in their uniform of blue serge with red piping and a little pill-box hat. The telegram itself came in an orange envelope, smaller than the average letter, the message in capital letters on ticker tape stuck on a half sheet of rather mealy paper.

In our family one did not send telegrams lightly, partly because they were expensive but more because one was fearful of the initial shock when the door opened on the telegraph boy, the immediate assumption always being that he brought bad news. This was a legacy of the First War when telegraph boys were over-employed. Bumping over the setts on their high bicycles, every day they brought news of deaths in the trenches so that a single boy in four years of war might tell the fate of thousands. Seeing him go by women would stand at their doors to see which house he stopped at, this pageboy of death. And the same, presumably, in Germany: *Der Todeskavalier*.

I thought once of writing a TV play about such a boy, who, with men being called up, heard in the autumn of 1914 that 'they were taking on down at the Post Office' and so goes and gets his first job. He becomes a telegraph boy for the two years before he himself is old enough to enlist, thus every day bringing tidings of the fate of others that he knows may one day be his own.

And finally, an apology. How dramatists use (and invariably sanitise) illness for their own purposes is an interesting subject. The illnesses change: a hundred years ago if a character needed to fade away it was with TB or 'consumption'. When fifty years or so ago TB ceased to be incurable it lost its popularity as a dramatic disease to be replaced very often by leukaemia, another condition with which a character could make a slow and dignified exit. That neither disease was as tidy or as well-mannered as dramatists chose to imagine seems insulting to the victims and now I am conscious that I have treated Francis's death in much the same way, deaths from AIDS seldom so quick or so clean as I have made his departure, my only excuse being that it is Violet's story more than his.

The six monologues were each rehearsed for just over a week and generally taped over one day at Twickenham Studios. I am grateful to all the performers, the directors and the production team whose names are separately listed and they will know that it is no reflection on them when I say that at every stage of the production process I never ceased to miss the presence of my long-time producer and friend, Innes Lloyd, who produced the first series of *Talking Heads* and who died in 1991. It is to him these monologues are dedicated.

THE HAND OF GOD

Celia · Eileen Atkins

CELIA, A MIDDLE-AGED WOMAN, SITS AT THE END OF A REFECTORY TABLE. THERE ARE ODD PLATES ON THE WALL, A GRANDFATHER CLOCK: THE CORNER OF AN ANTIQUE SHOP. IN THE COURSE OF THE MONOLOGUE CELIA SITS IN VARIOUS PARTS OF THE SHOP, OFTEN BY AN OIL RADIATOR.

I won't touch pictures. I make it a rule. I've seen too many fingers burned.

Woman comes in this morning starts rooting in her shopping bag saying she has something I might be interested in, been in the attic etcetera etcetera. The usual rigmarole. Hadn't thought anything about it, apparently, until she saw something similar on (and I knew what was coming) that television programme about antiques and that someone on the programme from Christie's...

I said, 'Barrow boys.' She said, 'Come again?' I said, 'Sotheby's, Christie's. Barrow boys. Nicely spoken, lovely suits, finger-nails immaculate. But barrow boys.' She said, 'Well anyway, he said £2000.'

I said, 'Well, he would. He doesn't have to get up at four in the morning and flog his ageing Volvo halfway across England just to sit all day in a freezing marquee and come away with two trivets and an umbrella-stand.' £2000! It was one step up from Highland cattle.

She said, 'It's a genuine oil painting. Look at the work that's gone into it.' I said, 'Madam, if you'll forgive me, could I point you along the street in the direction of A Tisket A Tasket? Basically a café it doubles as a bric-a-brac shop and Yvonne does pictures on the side...' though what I didn't say was that they tend to be mice in pinnies-type thing.

I popped over the road to tell Derek and Cyril. They'd just

had a buyer in from Stockholm who'd practically cleared them out. Staffordshire mostly, which is their big thing. Doesn't do anything for me but Derek and Cyril love it; chunky, I suppose. Actually I don't have a particular line. Good cottage furniture sums it up, elm, fruitwood and anything painted. And clocks, of course, when I can get hold of them. Plus pots of the period.

Some things I won't sell. Teddy bears, for instance. Teddy bears are a minefield. I was at a sale in Suffolk and saw a teddy bear actually torn apart between two bidders, one of them a vicar.

These days they're all going in for little sidelines. Eking the job out with jam and little pots of chutney. Woman came in the other day, said, Did I have any chutney? I said, 'I shall start doing chutney, madam, when Tesco start doing gateleg tables.' But the garage sells pot-pourri so what do you expect?

I think of Lawrence. 'Christ, old girl, I didn't sink my gratuity in this place to start selling bloody condiments.' He was in bomb disposal which was why to begin with we went in for clocks. Though of course there were clocks then. There was everything then. Furniture. Pottery. Stock no problem. And if one had the eye, which I do, one could pick and choose.

Not any more. Take what you can get. And money, money, money. If you love beautiful things, which is why I came into this business in the first place, it just breaks your heart.

And everybody's an expert now, up to all the tricks of the trade. You'll see something catch their eye and they don't ask about it straightaway; they enquire about something else, pretend they're not interested then it's, 'Oh… incidentally, how much is this little thing?' It's the oldest dodge in the world and they expect you to be taken in by it. Of course they've picked all that up off the television. I won't have one. I said to Nancy

Barnard, I refuse to watch. She said, 'Well, we only have it because of Fay.' Fay! They're both glued to it!

Wish I could shift this refectory table. It was a real snip when I got it but I've had it a year now and not a nibble. Lovely top. Elm.

She gives a little smile as someone obviously looks in the window.

Old Miss Ventriss seeing what there is. Took two Crown Derby plates off her once, just as a favour, one of them chipped.

Looking a bit frail. Going on.

Lovely cameo brooch.

FADE.

They talk as if you're not in the room.

Couple just now, looking at the Asiatic Pheasant tureen. '£60!' she said, 'I gave £2.10 for mine.' 'Yes, but when?' I wanted to say, '1955?'

And some of them so careless they practically hurl things to the floor. I've got a notice up now:

'Lovely to look at, nice to hold,
but if you break it
I say Sold!'

Somebody looking in. Goldfish bowl.

No. You can't see the price, however far you bend. You're going to dislocate your neck and you still won't see it, because I've carefully arranged the ticket so that if you want to see the price you'll have to come into the shop. Which you're not doing.

Even if they could see the price they wouldn't understand it because I've got my little code.

She looks at the ticket on the refectory table, at the end of which she's sitting.

I could take £1300 for this at a pinch. I've had it a year. Too long. Lawrence would be reading me the Riot Act. 'Keep your stock ticking over, old girl. Move it on.' And he did, even if it meant not making much.

'It's like Scrabble, my dear. Start saving up for the big one, the seven letter word, and you're done for. Get your letters down. £5 here. £10 there. Buy for x one week, sell for y the next. That's how you make your money.' Look well in a boardroom. Or one of these loft conversion things. I'd even consider £1150.

I kept wondering about Miss Ventriss. So what with not having seen her for a bit I thought I'd just knock on her door, see how she was.

She lives in one of the double-fronted houses on The Mount, original fanlight over the door and a lovely knocker, hand grasping a ball, which can't be later than 1820 though the house I'd have said was Victorian. But of course it's stucco which can cover a multitude of sins, and once I get inside I realise it's seventeenth century and seemingly never been touched. And I'm right, of course she isn't well, been in bed a fortnight and it's Mabel, the home help who answers the door. Now I know Mabel of old because she's been in from time to time with odd bits of stuff, little things...a silver vinaigrette, a jet brooch, spoons and whatnot, stuff I've found homes for straightaway. They all come from Newcastle, apparently, where her aunt's had to go into a home. Anyway Mabel takes me upstairs to see Miss Ventriss, who tells me she's had all sorts of tests and they still don't know what's wrong. Which probably means they do.

Thin little hand. Like dried leaves. Tragic.

Lovely bedside table with piecrust moulding. District Nurse comes while I'm there, plonks a bottle of medicine straight down on it. Criminal. I help give her some Benger's food only she fetches it straight back.

The spoon's silver and while they're cleaning her up I look at the hallmark. Provincial, Bristol, about 1830.

Same sort that Mabel brought in.

FADE.

I love a nice finish...maple, rosewood, and walnut particularly. What I can't abide is stripped pine. I don't see the point, quite frankly. And they're fanatics about it, some dealers. I mean still. They'll strip everything. Five minutes in the caustic tank and it's one hundred years of loving care down the drain. All the character gone.

I was thinking about this at Miss Ventriss's because there's polish everywhere. Walnut, elm, fruitwood. It's like a jewel box. I've been popping round on a regular basis lately, just to relieve Mabel a bit because the old girl's scarcely conscious now, doesn't know I'm there half the time. I sit by the bed with the clock ticking...carriage clock, tortoiseshell veneer, fluted, about 1750. Made me think of Lawrence. Lovely.

Of course, everywhere you look there's something. It's like houses used to be in the fifties, and most of it museum quality practically. It's from her grandfather, he was a great collector apparently.

I said to Mabel, 'What's going to happen to all this?' She said, Well she didn't think there were any relations. There'd been a niece in Canada but she had a feeling she was in an airline crash.

I couldn't get her to take me round at first. Said she was under strict instructions from the solicitors. I said, 'What solicitors are those?' She said, 'Paterson, Beatty and Brown.' I said, 'Well, there's no problem there because I took a kneehole desk off Mr Paterson and gave him a very good price.'

She was still a bit reluctant so I said, 'Mabel, I can well understand why you have to be careful. It's so easy for little things to go walkabout, particularly with old people. Silver, little brooches, you know the sort of thing?' She went a bit quiet so I said, 'Shall we start with upstairs?'

I couldn't believe it. Every room a treasure trove. Amazing.

When I was going Mabel said, 'I'll try and steer some of it your way if I can.' I said, 'Yes, well there'd be a nice little margin on most of this even running to the two of us. If the worst comes to the worst, of course.' Mabel says 'Yes. Though she seems a bit better today. Kept more of her dinner down anyway. Still, you've only to look at her under that nightdress and there's nothing there.' I said, 'Yes. Where did that nightdress come from?' She said 'Her grandmother, I think. It's all hand done. There's half a dozen of them in the linen cupboard, some of them never worn. Tragic.'

Of course the sharks are beginning to gather. I'm sitting by the bed this afternoon when Derek knocks at the door bearing one of Cyril's wizened egg custards. Mabel didn't let him get his foot round the door only then Nancy Barnard rolls up in her terrible beetroot slacks, says that she and Fay swear by some tincture from the swamps of Paraguay that they'd bought in Chelmsford, should she get her some? I said to Mabel, 'They're so transparent.'

Miss Ventriss is asleep so I have a little look at her bed. It's a country piece. About 1830 I'd have said, painted (which always gets my vote) and in such good condition. The doorbell goes again so while Mabel's downstairs I lift up the mattress and where the paint isn't worn it's as good as new.

I'm just tucking the sheet back when I see her little eyes are open and she's watching me. I think she said, 'Happy?' Only Mabel came in just then.

Of course you can't tell when it gets to this stage, it goes to the brain.

The visitor's the priest, come to anoint her and whatnot, just to be on the safe side, as the doctor says she could go any time. Mabel and I left him to it, just stood respectfully in the background. Had a little embroidered cloth that he covered the chalice with, Arts and Crafts by the look of it and a beautiful thing. Pity it can't be used for something.

Pause.

Of course, when she said 'Happy?', what she probably meant was that she was happy.

FADE.

I said to Nancy Barnard, 'Am I a person?' She said, 'Come again, love?' I said, 'Am I a person? Or am I simply a profess-ional bargain hunter?'

Because that was what she was implying. I said, 'I've been

coming here as a friend.' She said, 'I know that.' Bright red cardigan, carmine lipstick and, at the funeral, leather trousers. Even Nancy had managed to find a skirt. Niece...she'd never even met Miss Ventriss, went to Canada at the age of six. Mabel had given me to understand she'd died in an airline crash. Turns out what she'd had was a hairline fracture, no crash at all.

And of course she comes in for everything. Which is understandable, except that no sooner does she see the place than she announces that aside from one or two of the choicest pieces which she'd be keeping for herself, she'd be sending the rest to Phillips.

I said, 'Mrs O'Rourke, I'm sure there are several local concerns who'd give you a very good price and you wouldn't be landed with the vendor's commission.' Turns out she's not paying much commission anyway as the stuff is of such good quality she'd come to an arrangement.

It was then she offered me this box of odds and ends from the desk drawer...I'd been very kind to her aunt, she said, and she wanted to give me a bit of something in return.

I said, 'Thank you very much but I don't want to be given anything.' She said, 'That's good because with the solicitors being such sticklers I probably ought to charge you a nominal price anyway then it's all legal and above board. Shall we say £5? I said, 'I don't sell bric-a-brac.' She said, 'Well, if you give me £5 and it fetches more than that you can give the rest to Oxfam.' I said, 'What do you do in Canada?' She said, 'Public relations.' I said 'Oh' pointedly. 'You must be on holiday then,' gave her £5, took the box and went.

Of course being Canadian she probably thought I was being nice.

I haven't been able to face unpacking the box. In fact, I've only just done it now. Much as I expected. One or two pressed glass ashtrays that I can get £2 or £3 a piece for. A little gun-metal cigarette case and a serviette ring. All of them items for the oddments box. The only thing of any interest at all is a rather smudgy drawing of a finger (I think it's a drawing, it may be a print) but the frame is very distinctive. Quite small but with little doors that open so it looks a bit like an altar, nineteenth century probably.

When I've got a minute I'm going to take the drawing out and put something a bit more conventional in, a flower print or something. Smarten it up a bit. Might fetch £30 or so, you never know.

Pause.

Funny thing to put in a frame, a finger.

FADE.

I think the refectory table's gone. Came in this morning. Only young. Curly hair. Can't have been much more than twenty. I said, Was he looking for anything in particular? He said, Well, he did want a little present for his girlfriend but he was interested in the refectory table. Didn't begin by asking the price, which is always a good sign, just said could I measure it for him?

While I'm rooting about looking for a tape measure he picks up one or two bits and pieces. I'd brought Miss Ventriss's little drawing out thinking I could spend the afternoon taking it out of the frame, and I'd just popped it down on the refectory table where he picks it up, then puts it on one side so's he could look more closely at the table top.

When I'd measured it he got underneath and had a proper look; there was a bit of worm but in a piece that age it would be unusual if there wasn't and anyway we both thought it was dead. So he said, what was the best I could do? I'd given £1100 for it a year ago so I said, 'Well, I can't do much under £1700. Say £1650. It's elm.' He said, 'I know. It's beautiful. If it will fit, it's just what we're looking for.' So I give him my card and he writes down the measurements and he's going to ring back this afternoon.

Just as he's going he picks up the drawing again and says 'What is this?' I said, 'Well, it's a finger, isn't it?' He said, 'Yes. I'm not sure I like that, though it's a nice frame. How much is it?'

I thought, Well, it's an educated voice, I'll take a chance. I said, 'I can't really do it much under £100.' He put it down pretty smartish. I said, 'The frame alone's worth more than that.' He said, 'Yes, it's the frame I'm really interested in.'

I reckoned to look at my book. I said, 'Well, I can do it for £90 and if you're not particular for the drawing I can take it out.' He said, 'No, don't bother, I can do that.' And just then somebody comes in and he writes me out a cheque really quickly. I wrapped it up and said, 'And you'll let me know about the table?' He said, 'What?' I said, 'The table.' He said, 'Oh yes. I'll phone you this afternoon. I think it'll be just right.'

I've just popped along to the bank and put the cheque in and now I'm waiting for him to call. It's funny I'd come down to £90 but he was in such a rush he'd still made it out for £100.

FADE.

I said, No, I wasn't the sort of person who is resentful. I'd made my profit and they had made theirs. Selling on, everybody makes something, that's what the antique business is all about.

They'd posed me outside the shop and this young woman stood by the camera and I had to look at her and not at it.

She said, Would I be asking them to give me an ex gratia payment? I said, I didn't think I would be asking and I was sure they wouldn't be offering. Of course it would be nice if they did. I think I would...in the circumstances.

I'd actually forgotten all about it. It was six months ago at least (apparently they had a lot of tests to do on the paper and whatnot). Then Nancy Barnard comes banging on the window one morning before I'd even opened, holding up a copy of the *Telegraph* and pointing to this photograph on the front page. And there's the young man, and a blow-up of the finger.

Which, so all (or anyway some) of the experts say is by Michelangelo, a study (one of the few apparently) of the hand of God on the Sistine Chapel ceiling.

'I knew I'd seen it before,' Nancy says, 'only it was Fay who pointed it out. Glued to the telly box as usual she said it's like the finger they have at the start of the *South Bank Show*. Such a shame! If you watched the telly you might have known.'

What makes it special apparently is the ring. God doesn't have a ring on his finger on the ceiling, I mean why should he...but the ring on my...on the finger has, very faintly, the arms of the Pope who commissioned it... Julius something or other, who was Michelangelo's patron. Very satirical apparently on Michelangelo's part, though I don't see the joke.

But all of which, needless to say, bumps up the estimated

price. Not been sold yet but could fetch anything... £5 million, £10 million... unique.

A finger. That size.

'Poor you,' said Nancy. 'Oh,' I said, 'it happens.' Only when she'd gone I was physically sick.

The young man who bought it, whom I thought looked quite classy, turns out to be some young blood from Christie's. Says in the paper he picked it up in a junk shop. Junk shop.

Of course the person who ought to feel really sick is the niece, Mrs O'Rourke. I don't think she can ever have looked in the box so she'll have had no idea. So I've dropped her a line. Wipe the smile off her face.

Been quite busy. Mostly people just wanting a look. At me, chiefly.

Still, they've bought the odd thing. Sold a couple of lemonade bottles yesterday. Only my stock's low. Can't face going to sales yet. And I've still got this bloody refectory table.

Knee deep in tomatoes so I made some chutney. Frilly top. Italic label. 95p a bottle. Sold three this afternoon.

FADE.

MISS FOZZARD FINDS HER FEET

Miss Fozzard · Patricia Routledge

NONDESCRIPT SUBURBAN SITTING ROOM. IN THE COURSE OF THE MONOLOGUE MISS FOZZARD SITS ON VARIOUS CHAIRS OR STANDS BY THE FIREPLACE BUT THE SETTING IS THE SAME THROUGHOUT.

Bit of a bombshell today. I'm just pegging up my stocking when Mr Suddaby says, 'I'm afraid, Miss Fozzard, this is going to have to be our last encounter.' Apparently this latest burglary has put the tin hat on things and what with Mrs Suddaby's mother finally going into a home and their TV reception always being so poor there's not much to keep them in Leeds so they're making a bolt for it and heading off to Scarborough. Added to which Tina, their chow, has a touch of arthritis so the sands may help and the upshot is they've gone in for a little semi near Peasholme Park.

'But,' Mr Suddaby says, 'none of that is of any consequence. What is important, Miss Fozzard, is what are we going to do about your feet? You've been coming to me for so long I don't like to think of your feet falling into the wrong hands.'

I said, 'Well, Mr Suddaby, I shall count myself very lucky if I find someone as accomplished as yourself and, if I may say so, with your sense of humour.' Because it's very seldom we have a session in which laughter doesn't figure somewhere.

He said, 'Well, Miss Fozzard, chiropody is a small world and I've taken the liberty of making a few phone calls and come up with two possibilities. One is a young lady over in Roundhay, who, I understand is very reasonable.'

'A woman?' I said, 'In chiropody? Isn't that unusual?'
'No,' he said, 'not nowadays. The barriers are coming down in chiropody as in everything else. It's progress Miss Fozzard, the march of, and Cindy Bickerton has her own salon.' I said, 'Cindy? That doesn't inspire confidence. She sounds as if she should be painting nails not cutting them.'

'Well,' he said, 'in that case the alternative might be more up your street. I don't know him personally but Mr Dunderdale has got all the right letters after his name. He's actually retired but he still likes to take on a few selected clients, just to keep his hand in. However he does live out at Lawnswood and unless I'm very much mistaken you're not motorised?' I said, 'No problem. I can just bob on the 17. It's a bus I like. No, if it's all the same to you and the Equal Opportunities Board I'll opt for Mr Dunderdale.' He said, 'I think it's a wise decision. Allow me,' (and he winked) 'Allow me,' he said, 'to shake hands with your feet.'

I've been going to Mr Suddaby for years. I think it's an investment, particularly if you're like me and go in for slim-fitting court shoes (squeeze, squeeze). Mr Suddaby reads me the riot act, of course, but as he says, 'It's a free country, Miss Fozzard. If you want to open the door to a lifetime of hard skin, I can't stop you.' What view this Mr Dunderdale will take remains to be seen.

When I get back Mrs Beevers has her hat and coat on, can't wait to get off. Says Bernard has been propped up in a chair staring at the TV all evening. She helps me get him upstairs and then I sit by the bed and, as per the recovery programme, give him a run-down on my day.

Mr Clarkson-Hall down at the Unit says that when somebody has had a cerebral accident, 'In lay terms, a stroke, Miss Fozzard, we must take care not to treat them like a child. If your brother is going to recover his faculties, dear lady, the more language one can throw at him the better.'

I was just recounting my conversation with Mr Suddaby and how they're decamping to Scarborough when Bernard suddenly throws back his head and yawns.

I rang Mr Clarkson-Hall this morning. He says that's progress.

Pause.

I do miss work.

FADE.

I'm just getting my things on to go up to Mr Dunderdale's this evening, when Bernard has a little accident and manages to broadcast the entire contents of his bladder all the way down the stairs. Mrs Beevers is taking her time coming and it's only when I've got him all cleaned up and sitting on the throne that the doorbell eventually goes. Except even then it's not her, just a couple from church about Rwanda. I said, 'Never mind Rwanda, can we deal with the matter in hand and get a middle-aged gentleman off the lavatory?' So we get him downstairs and manoeuvre him onto his chosen chair five inches from the TV screen.

After they've gone I said, 'You can work the remote; it's about time you remembered how to wipe your own bottom.' Not a flicker. Of course, that's where they have you with a stroke: you never know what goes in and what doesn't.

When Mrs Beevers eventually does roll up she's half an hour late which means I've missed the ten past and have to run all the way up Dyneley Road so by the time I'm ringing Mr Dunderdale's doorbell I'm all flustered and very conscious that my feet may be perspiring. He said, 'Well if that is what is troubling you, Miss Fozzard, I can straightaway put paid to the problem because I always kick off the proceedings by applying a mild astringent.'

Refined-looking feller, seventy-odd but with a lovely head

of hair, one of the double-fronted houses that look over the cricket field. Rests my foot on a large silk handkerchief which I thought was a civilised touch; Mr Suddaby just used to use yesterday's *Evening Post*.

He said, 'Well, Miss Fozzard, I take one look at these and I say to myself here is someone who is on her feet a good deal. Am I right?' I said, 'You are. I'm in charge of the soft furnishing department at Matthias Robinson's, or was until my brother was taken ill. Anything you want in cretonne you know where to come.' He said, 'I might hold you to that but meanwhile could I compliment you on your choice of shoe.' I said, 'Well, as a rule I steer clear of suede because as a shoe it's a bit high maintenance, but sometimes I think the effort with the texturiser pays dividends.' He said, 'I can see we share a philosophy. If I may, I'll just begin by clipping your toenails.'

He said, 'Of course as soon as you walked in I picked you out as a professional woman.' I said, 'How?' He said, 'By your discreet choice of accessories.' I said, 'Well I favour a conservative approach to fashion, peppy but classic if you know what I mean.' He said, 'I do. There's been a verruca here, but it's extinct. Do you know why I chose the profession of chiropody?' I said, 'No.' He said, 'It's so that I could kneel at the feet of thousands of women and my wife would never turn a hair.' I said, 'Oh. Is there a Mrs Dunderdale?' He said, 'There was. She passed over.'

When he'd finished he rubbed in some mentholated oil (Moroccan apparently) and said I'd just feel a mild tingling effect which wasn't unpleasant and said my feet were in tip top condition, the only possible cloud on the horizon a pre-fungal condition between two of my toes that he wanted to keep a watchful eye on.

Had on a lovely cardigan. I said, 'I hope you'll excuse me asking but is that cardigan cashmere?' He said, 'Well spotted, Miss Fozzard. This may be the first time you've seen it but it won't be the last, could I offer you a glass of sweet sherry?'

Churchwarden at St Wilfred's apparently, past president of the Inner Wheel and nicely off by the looks of it, a pillar of the community. When he's at the door he says, 'Next time, if you're very good, I shall initiate you into the mysteries of the metatarsal arch.'

I thought about it on the bus and when I gave Mrs Beevers her money I told her that with my wanting to get back to work she'd no need to come again as I was going to advertise for someone permanent. Bernard's got a bit put by and if this isn't a rainy day I don't know what is.

He was watching TV so I switched it off and took him through my evening as Mr Clarkson-Hall said I should. He looked a bit snotty but I said 'Bernard, nobody ever learned to talk again by watching the snooker.' Told him about Mr Dunderdale and the pre-fungal condition between my toes, his cashmere cardigan and whatnot.

As Mr Clarkson-Hall says, 'Miss Fozzard, it doesn't matter what you say so long as it's language: language is balls coming at you from every angle.' And it's working. I'd got him into bed and was just closing the door when I heard him say his first word. I think it was 'cow'.

When I rang Mr Clarkson-Hall to tell him he said, 'Why cow?' I said, 'Probably an advert on TV.'

Still he agreed: it's a breakthrough.

FADE.

It was just that bit warmer today so I thought if I went along in my mustard Dannimac I could team it with my ancient peep-toe sandals that haven't had an airing since last summer when I had a little run over to Whitby with Joy Poyser.

Well, Mr Dunderdale couldn't get over them. Said he'd not seen a pair like them in fifteen years and that in the support they gave to the instep plus the unimpeded circulation of air via the toe no more sensible shoe had ever been devised. Made me parade up and down the room in them and would have taken a photograph only he couldn't put his hands on his Polaroid. Anyway I'm taking them along so that we can do it next time.

Wants me to go fortnightly until my tinea pedis yields to treatment but he's going to do it for the same fee and now that I'm back at work and we've got Miss Molloy coming in to see to Bernard there's no problem.

She said, 'Call me Mallory.' I said, 'Mallory? What sort of name is that? I wouldn't be able to put a sex to it.' She says, 'Well, I'm Australian.' Strong girl, very capable. And a qualified physiotherapist with a diploma in caring. It's Australian caring but I suppose it'll be the same as ours only minus the bugbear of hypothermia.

Ideally I would have preferred someone older, or someone less young anyway only we weren't exactly inundated with applicants which surprised me because I'd have thought it would have been a nice little sideline for a pensioner, though they'd have to be able-bodied. She chucks Bernard about as if he's two ha-porth of copper. Hails from Hobart, Tasmania, originally; I suppose England offers more scope for caring than the bush. And she and Bernard seem to hit it off, says she likes his sense of humour. I said to Joy Poyser, 'News to me. I didn't know he had one.'

Mind you, it's bearing fruit as movement's certainly

coming back, he can hop up and down stairs now, more or less under his own steam. Speech too, because of course with him having company all day he gets the practice.

I was telling the whole saga of the stroke to Mr Dunderdale as he was tackling a patch of hard skin. He said, 'What did Bernard do, Miss Fozzard? I said, 'Not to put too fine a point on it, Mr Dunderdale, he was a murderer. He said, 'Oh. That's unusual.' I said, 'Well, he was a tobacconist which comes to the same thing. Sweets and tobacco, a little kiosk in Headingley.' He said, 'Yes, well sweets and tobacco…it's a lethal combination.' I said, 'He smoked, he was overweight and he certainly liked a drink. Worry is another cause, I know, but as I said to Mr Clarkson-Hall that is something he never did. But now, of course he's paying for it. Only what seems unfair is that I'm paying for it too.'

Mr Dunderdale looked up and he said, 'Yes' (and he had my foot in his hand). He said, 'Yes. If there had been thirteen disciples instead of twelve, the other one would have been you Miss Fozzard'.

Green silk handkerchief this time. Last week it was red.

The words are beginning to come back, though, no doubt about it and when he can't manage a word I get him to do what Mr Clarkson-Hall suggested, namely describe what he means and skirt a path round it. Miss Molloy makes him do it as well and she says one way and another they get along. Bathes him every day, rubs him with baby oil, says that where bedsores are concerned prevention is better than cure.

I still go in on a night and give him all my news. Mr Dunderdale had been saying that it was a pity evolution had taken the turn that it did because if it hadn't we might have found ourselves making as much use of our feet as we do our hands, which in the present economic climate might have been just what's needed to tip the balance. Miss Molloy said, 'That's interesting,' only Bernard just groans.

Personally I'm surprised she can put up with him but she says that by Australian standards he's a gentleman.

I hear them laughing.

FADE.

Soft Furnishings, we're always a bit slack first thing so I'll generally do a little wander over into Floor Coverings and have a word with Estelle Metcalf. I wish it was Housewares we were next to as that would make it Joy Poyser because Estelle's all right but she's a bit on the young side, big glasses, boy friend's one of these who dress up as cavaliers at the weekend.

I said to her this morning, 'Shiatsu.' She said, 'Come again?' I said, 'Shiatsu, what is it?' She said, 'Is it a tropical fish?' I said, 'No.' She said, 'Is it a mushroom?' I said, 'No.' She said, 'Is it Mr Dunderdale?' I said, 'Why should it be Mr Dunderdale?' She said, 'Because most things are with you these days.' I said, 'I shall ignore that, Estelle. Suffice it to say it's a form of massage involving various pressure points on the body that was invented by the Japanese.' She said, 'That's all very well but it didn't stop them doing Pearl Harbour, did it?' Neville's besieging York on Sunday, trying out his new breast-plate. Estelle's going along as an imploring housewife who comes out under a flag of truce.

Just then a customer comes in wanting some seersucker slipovers so we had to cut it short. I don't talk about Mr Dunderdale. And if I do she talks about Oliver Cromwell.

I go weekly now, though Mr Dunderdale won't charge me

any more. I was sat on the sofa afterwards while he put away his instruments and he said, 'Good news, Miss Fozzard. We seem to have cracked the *tinea pedis*, not a trace of it left. I think that calls for a sherry refill. Are you in a hurry to get off?' I said, 'No. Why?' He said, 'Well, we still have a little time in hand and I wonder if I might prevail upon you to try on a pair of bootees?' I said, 'Bootees?'

He said, 'Well, I'm using the term loosely. They're technically what we would call a fur-lined Gibson bruised look but bootees is a convenient shorthand. The shade is Bengal bronze.' I said, 'Well, they're a lovely shoe.' He said, 'Yes. Cosy, ankle-hugging they make a beautiful ending to the leg. They're a present, of course.' I said, 'Oh, Mr Dunderdale, I couldn't.' He said, 'Miss Fozzard, please. My contacts in the world of footwear procure me a considerable discount. Besides there is a little something you can do for me in return.' I said, 'Oh?' He said, 'My years in bending over ladies' feet have resulted in an intermittently painful condition of the lower back which, if you are amenable you have it in your power to alleviate.' I said, 'I do, Mr Dunderdale?' He said, 'You do, Miss Fozzard. I'm going to put one cushion on the hearthrug here for my head and the other here for my abdomen and now I'm going to lie down and what I want you to do is to step on my lower back.' I said, 'Should I take the bootees off?' He said, 'No, no. Keep the bootees on – their texture makes them ideal for the purpose. That's it. Steady yourself by holding onto the edge of the mantelpiece if you want.'

Then he said something I couldn't hear because his face was pressed into the carpet. 'What was that, Mr Dunderdale?' 'I said, "Excellent," Miss Fozzard. You may move about a little if you would care to.' I said, 'I'm anxious not to hurt you,

Mr Dunderdale.' He said, 'Have no fears on that score, Miss Fozzard. Trample away.' I said, 'I feel like one of those French peasants treading the grapes.' He said, 'Yes. Yes, yes.' I said, 'Do you feel the benefit?' He said, 'Yes, yes, I do. Thank you. If you don't mind, Miss Fozzard I'll just lie here for a little while. Perhaps you could see yourself out.'

So I just left him on the hearthrug.

When I got back Bernard is sitting on the sofa with Miss Molloy, both of them looking a bit red in the face. 'We were just laughing,' Miss Molloy says, 'because Bernard couldn't think of a word.' 'Well,' I said, 'he must learn to skirt round it.' 'Oh, he did that all right,' she said. 'You're an expert at that, aren't you Bernard?' And they both burst out laughing.

Mr Clarkson-Hall's very pleased with him. Says he's never known a recovery so quick. Says he didn't have the privilege of knowing Bernard before but he imagines he's now quite like his old self. I said, 'Yes. He is.'

After Miss Molloy had gone he comes in here while I'm having my hot drink and says he's thinking of opening the kiosk again and that Mallory is going to help him. I said, 'Does Miss Molloy have any experience of sweets and tobacco?' He said, 'No, but she's a fun-loving girl with a welcoming whatever it's called and that's half the battle.'

Note from Mr Dunderdale this morning saying his back is much better and that he was looking forward to seeing me next week.

Estelle suffers in the back department, the legacy from once having had to wield a spare pike at the Battle of Naseby. So I was telling her all about me helping Mr Dunderdale with his, only she wasn't grateful. Just giggles and says, 'Ooh, still waters!'

Floor coverings, they ought to have somebody more mature. She really belongs in Cosmetics.

FADE.

I don't know what's got into people at work. I come in this morning and the commissionaire with the moustache who's on the staff door says, 'Have a good day, my duck.' I said, 'You may only have one arm, Mr Capstick, but that doesn't entitle you to pat me on the bottom. Next thing is I'm invoicing some loose covers in Despatch when one of the work experience youths who can't be more than sixteen gives me a silly wink.

I said to Estelle, 'My Viyella two-piece doesn't normally have this effect.' She said, 'Well they're just wanting to be friendly.' I said, 'Friendly? Estelle, I may not be a feminist (though I did spearhead the provision of pot-pourri in the ladies toilets) but people are not going to pat my bottom with impunity.' Estelle says, 'No. The boot's on the other foot,' and starts giggling. I said to Joy Poyser, 'How ever she manages to interest anyone in serious vinyl flooring I do not understand.'

House dark when I got in. I imagine they're in the sitting room, the pair of them only I call out and there's no sound. So I get my tea and read the *Evening Post*, nice to have the place to myself for a change.

Then I go into the sitting room and there's Bernard sitting there in the dark. I put the light on and he's got the atlas open. I said, 'What are you doing in the dark?' He said, 'Looking up the Maldive Islands.' 'Why,' I said, 'you're not going on holiday?' He said, 'No, I'm not. How can I go on bloody holiday? What with?' And he shoves a bank statement at me.

I've a feeling he's been crying and I'm not sure where to

put myself so I go put the kettle on while I look at his statement. There's practically nothing in it, money taken out nearly every day. I said, 'What's this?' He said, 'It's that tart from Hobart.' I said, 'Miss Molloy? But she's a qualified physiotherapist.' He said, 'Yes and she's something else...she's a – what do you call it – female dog.'

I said, 'Did you sign these cheques?' He said, 'Of course I signed them.' I said, 'What were you doing, practising writing?' He said, 'No.' I said, 'Where is she?' He said, 'The Maldive Islands, where I was going to be.' I said, 'Well we must contact the police. It's fraud is this.' He said, 'No it isn't.' I said, 'What did you think these cheques were for?' He said, 'I knew what they were for. For services rendered. And I don't mean lifting me on and off the what's it called. It's stuff she did for me.' I said, 'What stuff?' He said, 'You know.'

I said, 'Remember what Mr Clarkson-Hall says, Bernard. Trace a path round the word.' He said, 'I don't have to trace a path round the bloody word. I know the word. It's you that doesn't. You don't know bloody nothing.' I said, 'Well one thing is plain. Despite your cerebral accident your capacity for foul language remains unimpaired.' He said, 'You're right. It bloody does.'

I made him some tea. I said, 'She's made a fool of you.' Bernard said, 'You can speak.' I said, 'You mean talk. I know

I can speak. The expression is, you can talk. Anyway why?' He said, 'Monkeying about with your foot feller.' I said, 'Mr Dunderdale? What's he got to do with it?' He said, 'Little games and whatnot. He's obviously a...a...' I said, 'A what?' He said, 'A...thing.' I said, 'Skirt a path round the word, Bernard. A what?' He said, 'Skirt it yourself you stupid...four legs, two horns, where you get milk.' I said, 'Cow. You normally remember that.'

I was telling Joy Poyser about it and she said, 'Well, why did you tell him about the chiropodist?' I said, 'Mr Clarkson-Hall said that I should talk to him, it's part of the therapy.' She said, 'It's not part of the therapy for Estelle Metcalf, is it? You told her. She's not had a stroke.' Apparently she's spread it all over the store.'

Anyway I came upstairs, left him crying over the atlas, when suddenly I hear a crash. I said, 'Bernard? Bernard?'

Pause.

'Bernard!'

FADE.

Estelle ventured into Soft Furnishings yesterday, first time for a week. Testing the water, I suppose. Said Neville was taking part in the battle of Marston Moor on Sunday. She's going along as a camp follower but they're short of one or two dishevelled Roundhead matrons and was I interested? I said, 'It's kind of you to offer, Estelle, but I think from now I'd be well advised to keep a low profile.'

People don't like to think you have a proper life, that's what I've decided. Or any more of a life than they know about. Then when they find out they think it's shocking. Else funny. I never thought I had a life. It was always Bernard who had the life.

He's worse this time than the last. Eyes used to follow you then. Not now. Log. Same rigmarole, though. Talk to him. Treat him like a person. Not that he ever treated me like a person. Meanwhile Madam is laid out on the beach in the

Maldives. He was on the rug when I found him. Two inches the other way and he'd have hit his head on the fender. Lucky escape.

I'd written to Mr Dunderdale, cancelling any further appointments. I didn't say why, just that with Bernard being poorly again it wasn't practical anyway. Which it wasn't.

So it was back to normal, sitting with Bernard, doing a few little jobs. I'd forgotten how long an evening could be.

Anyway, I was coming away from work one night and a big browny-coloured car draws up beside me, the window comes down and blow me if it isn't Mr Dunderdale.

He said, 'Good evening, Miss Fozzard. Could I tempt you up to Lawnswood? I'd like a little chat.' I said, 'Could we not talk here?' He said, 'Not in the way I'd like. I'm on a double yellow line.' So I get in and he runs me up there and whatever else you can say about him he's a very accomplished driver.

Anyway he sits me down in his study and gives me a glass of sherry and says why did I not want to come and see him any more. Well, I didn't know what to say. I said, 'It isn't as if I don't look forward to my appointments.' He said, 'Well, dear lady, I look forward to them too.' I said, 'But now that I have to get help in for Bernard again I can't afford to pay you.'

He said, 'Well, may I make a suggestion? Why don't we reverse the arrangement?' I said, 'Come again.' He said, 'Do it vice versa. I pay you.' I said, 'Well, it's very unusual.' He said, 'You're a very unusual woman.' I said, 'I am? Why?' He said, 'Because you're a free spirit, Miss Fozzard. You make your own rules.' I said, 'Well, I like to think so.' He said, 'I'm the same. We're two of a kind, you and I, Miss Fozzard. Mavericks. Have you ever had any champagne?' I said, 'No, but I've seen it at the conclusion of motor races.' He said, 'Allow me. To the future?'

It's all very decorous. Quite often he'll make us a hot drink and we'll just sit and turn over the pages of one of his many books on the subject, or converse on matters related. I remarked the other day how I'd read that Imelda Marcos had a lot of shoes. He said, 'She did...and she suffered for it at the bar of world opinion, in my view, Miss Fozzard, unjustly.'

Little envelope on the hall table as I go out, never mentioned, and if there's been anything beyond the call of duty there'll be that little bit extra. Buys me no end of shoes, footwear generally. I keep thinking where's it all going to end but we'll walk that plank when we come to it.

I've never had the knack of making things happen. I thought things happened or they didn't. Which is to say they didn't. Only now they have...sort of.

Bernard gets an attendance allowance now and what with that and the envelopes from Mr Dunderdale I can stay on at work and still have someone in to look after him. Man this time. Mr Albright. Pensioner, so he's glad of a job. Classy little feller, keen on railways and reckons to be instigating Bernard into the mysteries of chess. Though Mr Albright has to play both sides of course.

At one point I said to Mr Dunderdale, 'People might think this rather peculiar particularly in Lawnswood.' He said, 'Well, people would be wrong. We are just enthusiasts, Miss Fozzard, you and I and there's not enough enthusiasm in the world these days. Now if those Wellingtons are comfy I just want you in your own time and as slowly as you like very gently to mark time on my bottom.'

Occasionally he'll have some music on. I said once, 'I suppose that makes this the same as aerobics.' He said, 'If you like.'

It's droll but the only casualty in all this is my feet, because nowadays the actual chiropody gets pushed to one side a bit. If I want an MOT I really have to nail him down.

We're still Mr Dunderdale and Miss Fozzard and I've not said anything to anybody at work. Learned my lesson there.

Anyway, people keep saying how well I look.

Pause.

I suppose there's a word for what I'm doing but...I skirt round it.

FADE.

PLAYING SANDWICHES

Wilfred · David Haig

A MIDDLE-AGED MAN IN THE BASIC UNIFORM (DONKEY JACKET, NAVY BLUE OVERALLS) OF A PARKS ATTENDANT. HE SITS AGAINST THE PLANKS OF A PARK SHELTER, PAINTED BUT WORN AND COVERED WITH GRAFFITI.

I was in the paper shop this dinnertime getting some licorice allsorts. Man serving me said, 'I wish I was like you.' Shouted out to the woman, 'I wish I was him. Always buying sweets, never gets fat.' I said, 'Yes, I'm lucky. Only I cycle.' She said, 'Yes, I've seen you. You work for the Parks Department.' He said, 'Weren't you a lollipop man once?' I said, 'No.' He said, 'I thought I'd seen you, stood at the crossing.' Racks and racks of magazines. Always men in there, looking.

Janet was dressmaking, doing the twins' christening frocks. I said, 'They put on you, Janet. Before these frocks there's been no word for long enough.' She said, 'Well, whose fault is that?' Apricot satin, little buttons down the front.

Mr Trickett nosing round this afternoon at what he calls 'grassroots level' ordains a blitz on the bushes behind the playground. Privet mostly, all stinking of urine and clogged up with every sort of filth...sheaths; jamrags; a shoe; some tights; sick; dog muck. They come over the wall on a night after The Woodman's turned out, lie down drunk in all that filth and stench and do it. They do it in the playground too, laid down over one end of the slide where the kiddies slide along with their bottoms, then just chuck the evidence down anywhere.

I'm nearly finished when Mr Kumar stops with his barrow and brushes and we walk back to the yard together. He's from Bombay so he takes all this filth in his stride. Born a street sweeper, apparently, what they call an untouchable, though he's very neat, you'd never think it. Going on about getting his wife over from India. Got some decent digs in the Brudenells only a person from Liverpool comes and kicks the door in in the middle of the night. Thinks the English don't like the Indians; says the only Indians the English like are the Gurkhas. The Gurkhas cut people's heads off so that makes them the salt of the earth.

As we're going by the office Mr Parlane calls me in and says he's heard from Wakefield but they still can't trace my records. Foreman, dinner supervisor, lollipop man, I must have left some trace, was I sure I'd got all the digits right? I reeled the number off again and he said, 'Well, I'll try Pontefract, Wilfred, but it's been six months now.'

I went the long way round, pushing the bike. Just one kiddy by herself on the swings. Kiddy black. Mother, white, having a cig, watching.

FADE.

Against anonymous wallpaper; a bedroom, say.

I don't like a cargo of relations; I never have. I wasn't particular to go to the christening only Janet wanted to see what her frocks looked like on and anyway, as she said, who are Barry and Yvonne to look down their nose, their Martin's been had up twice for drunken driving.

Slight hiccup round the font because, since Martin hasn't actually managed to turn up they're short of a godfather. Yvonne wants to go ahead without but the young lad who's in charge says that though he personally is very relaxed about it, the church does tend to insist on there being a full complement of godparents.

We're all standing round looking a bit stumped when little Rosalie, who's seven, pipes up and says, 'Why can't Uncle Wilfred be it, he's my godfather.' Barry straight off clouts her only the priest who doesn't look much more than seventeen and new to the parish says, 'Would Uncle Wilfred be a possible solution?' I don't say anything at all only Yvonne gets in quick, 'No, Wilfred wouldn't be a possible solution because...' and Janet looks at her '...because they're not currently motorised.' The priest lad looks as if he's about to say that wheels aren't part of the job description when Yvonne spots Grandpa Greenwood who's just been out to spend a penny and says, 'He'll do'. The priest says, 'Isn't he a bit on the old side?' Yvonne says, 'No he isn't. He still goes ballroom dancing.' So it ends up being him. I said to Janet, 'At least baby Lorraine won't have any problems with the Military Twostep.'

Afterwards we adjourn to Sherwood Road where Pete and Gloria had laid something on, beer chiefly by the looks of it, one of those dos where the women end up in one room and the men in another. There are kiddies all over the place, though, and what with Pete's alsatian plunging around, sheer bedlam. That's irresponsible in my view, a dog that size when there are kiddies about. One snap and they're scarred for life. A lot of larking about with the children, Barry throwing their two up in the air till they screamed then pretends to throw one to me but doesn't. Ginger tash. Big fingers. Does a bit of decorating now and again, was in a remand home when he was young.

Then Pete starts telling his so-called jokes. 'Now then, which would you rather have, Wilf, a thousand women with one pound or one woman with a thousand pound?' 'Else neither,' says Barry and I saw him wink but I didn't take on. I thought I'd go and help wash up only no sooner were all the women in the kitchen when Janet has to embark on the saga of her womb, how we could have had children only the angle of it was wrong. So Yvonne chips in, 'It's not your angle, love, it's his that matters.' So there's a lot of smutty laughter and I go out and sit on the back step.

Little Rosalie's playing in the yard, throwing her ball against the wall, clapping her hands and lifting her leg to throw the ball under, all that. When she stops she comes and sits on the step and I say, 'I think that deserves a sweet, Rosalie,' and give her a licorice allsort. Suddenly there's a banging in the window and Yvonne bursts through the door and gets hold of the kiddy 'I told you, madam,' starts laying into her, and clawing the sweet out of her mouth. The dog's barking, the kiddy's crying, the old man has an accident and they're all shouting. So anyway we came away.

Janet doesn't say anything. Only when we're at the bus stop she says 'I don't want to have to be flitting again. If you made a decision never to buy any more licorice allsorts it would be a step in the right direction.'

So anyway, I promised.

FADE.

The edge of a bandstand, some wrought iron, but scribbled over and defaced.

Anybody that wants to make a fortune should invent something that'll erase the stuff they write up. There's a plaque on the wall by the fountain:

This park was opened on July 17 1936 by the
Rt. Honourable the Earl of Harewood KG. TD.

'So eat shit' some bright spark has sprayed across it, with the result I'm down there all morning with the Brasso and a wire brush.

'Think of it as a labour of love, Mr Paterson,' Parlane said. 'The present one's the music-lover.' 'Who?' 'The Earl of Harewood. Father married the old Princess Royal.' He hangs about for a bit then eventually says, Had I got a minute and he hoped I wouldn't take it amiss but had I been in prison? I said, 'No. What would I have been in prison for?' He said, He'd no idea, it was just that when records go walkabout as mine plainly had that was often the case.

I said, Well, it's not the case in this case, thank you very much and was my work unsatisfactory? He said, 'Far from it, the place has never been so tidy. You, Mr Paterson are a text-book example of why we went performance related. But you're also an example of somebody who has eluded all the fielders and ended up in the long grass, bureaucratically speaking. Well, don't worry. Gordon Parlane is going to make it his personal mission to retrieve you.'

It started spitting this afternoon so I thought I'd keep out of the rain and sweep up the bandstand. Young woman there again, the kiddy; I've seen them once or twice now, poor-looking, eating chips out of a carton.

She says, 'Are we all right sitting here?' I said, 'That's what it's for, visitors.' She said, 'We often come. The council's put us in bed and breakfast only the hotel's got proper people too and they don't like us around during the day. Samantha hates it, don't you Samantha?' The kiddy comes over and offers me a chip. 'You're privileged,' the mother says, 'she's frightened of men generally. Won't go near her father. Mind you, neither will I.'

Bonny little thing, only her mother's put her some

earrings in, stud things. And one in her little nose and she can't be more than seven. I wonder the law lets them do it, because that's interference in my view, ornamenting your kiddies, hanging stuff on them as if they were Christmas trees.

I'm sweeping up the rubbish and pretend to sweep up the kiddy too so she starts screaming with laughter. 'Oh,' her mother says, 'I think you've clicked. What is this place?' I said, 'What place?' 'This. This shelter thing.' I said, 'It's a bandstand. The band used to play here once upon a time.' She said, 'What band? You mean like a group?'

The kiddy came and stood by my knee. 'Yes,' I said. She said, 'Where did the fans go then? In the bushes?' She laughed and the kiddy laughed and put her hand on my leg. I said, 'It's stopped raining, I'd better get on.' She threw the chip carton down. She said, 'We'll see you. Wave to the man, Samantha. Wave.'

As I'm pushing the barrow back there's a policeman hanging about the fountain. Said he was just showing the flag and he'd be obliged if I'd keep my eye open for any undesirable elements. I said, 'Drugs, you mean?'

He said, 'Drugs or whatever. Men sitting too long on the benches type thing. Parks make for crime. This beat's a bugger.' As he was going he said, 'Pardon my asking but didn't you use to work at the Derby Baths?' I said, 'No, why?' He said, 'Nothing, the face is familiar. My two both got their bronze medal there. Well, I won't detain you, particularly since our Asian friend appears to be waiting.'

Pushing his barrow back Mr Kumar's all smiles because his wife has arrived. 'They took all her clothes off at the airport but otherwise,' he says, 'it was all as easy as falling off a log. I am a very happy man.'

'They're sly,' Janet said. 'Probably wants your job.' I said, 'What for?' 'His brother, his uncle, his nephew. They're all the same. Anyway I got my promotion. Same grade now as I was before. Keep this up a bit longer, Wilfred, and we might be able to run to a car again soon.'

FADE.

Planks again or municipal bricks. An outside wall, say.

Bit of excitement this morning. Body in the bushes. Little lad found it looking for his ball. Old man, one of the winos probably. Two police cars, an ambulance and more fuss made of him dead than there ever was alive. The child not worried at all, the mother hysterical. All over by half past ten and we were soon back in go mode, drizzle included.

I was heading for the tennis courts, trying to steer clear of the bandstand only Trickett shouts after me, 'Paterson. I don't want you skulking back there. The bandstand's in a disgusting state.'

Somebody'd thrown up all over the seat and I'd just about got it cleared up when the girl's calling out and the kiddy comes running in waving her little pink plastic handbag thing. 'Samantha's got you a present, haven't you Samantha. Give it to Mr...what's your name?' The child was putting her arms out to be lifted up.

'Hargreaves,' I said. 'My name's Hargreaves.' 'Give it to him Samantha,' and she takes out a daffodil from her little handbag and we put it in my buttonhole. 'She picked it herself,' the mother said. 'My name's Debbie.'

They sit watching while I go on cleaning up. She said,

'You're a bit too nice for this job aren't you? You look as if you should be doing something more up-market, a traffic warden or something.'

I said I liked being outside. The kiddy was pretending to help me sweep up again. 'It didn't used to be like this,' I said, 'all scribbled over and stuff written up.' 'Oh,' she says, 'I like the lived in look. Cans and litter and all that. You don't want it too clinical. Anyway it's all litter basically isn't it...Leaves is litter. Soil. We like it, don't we Samantha?'

I said, 'Why did you put them earring things in?' She said 'Her studs? Well, I don't see why she shouldn't have all the advantages other kids have. She's as good as anybody else. Don't you like them?' I said, 'No, Debbie. I do like them.'

After a bit the mother says Did I like her. I said Why? She said, 'Well we keep running into one another.' I said, 'You won't have Samantha tattooed, will you?' 'Oh no,' she said, 'not until she's old enough to make her own decisions. It's part of her life choices isn't it? Did the fountain used to go?' I said, 'Yes. When I was a boy. The fountain went. The band played. People kept off the grass. It was lovely.'

Mr Kumar comes by and says I have to call in at the office when it's convenient. He smiles at the girl but she doesn't take on. 'I don't care for Asians,' she said when he's gone. 'Neither one thing nor the other in my opinion.'

I went along to the office straightaway only it turns out to be nothing. Parlane has got some new idea about chasing me up on the computer. He said, 'I'm going to fax all your details over to Thorpe Arch, tell them Wakefield has been playing silly buggers (which they're always happy to hear) and get them as a personal favour to me to beam you up nationally. And if that doesn't work even Gordon Parlane is going to have to admit defeat.'

Coming out I ran into Mr Trickett. 'Oh,' he said spotting my buttonhole, 'Picking flowers now, Paterson?' I said somebody'd broken it off. He said, 'I don't know why we bother. They don't want gardens, they want their hands chopping off. I'd decapitate them let alone the bloody daffodils.' 'Anyway,' he said, 'Get rid of it. It sends the wrong message.'

They were still hanging about when I went back. 'Mr Hargreaves has lost his buttonhole,' Debbie said and the kiddy starts crying only when I pick her up she stops.

On the way home I called in at the sweetshop.

FADE.

Some sort of institutional background, half green, half cream. Wilfred is unshaven, with no tie on.

Janet's just been down, apparently. Left a clean vest and stuff at the desk. They said she wasn't allowed to speak to me at this stage; she said she didn't want to anyway.

It was the rain that did it because I'd given the bandstand a wide berth all week only Trickett comes into the yard this morning saying it was all flooded and wasn't that typical, one drop of rain and the place grinds to a halt. Tells me to get some rods and try and locate the problem. So I trundle over there and it's one of the grates that's stopped up. And I'm just getting my arm down to feel what the stoppage was when Samantha comes running along by the railings and puts her little face through the bars.

I said, 'Hello. Are you in prison?' She said, 'No. I've got an umbrella.' And she shows me her baby umbrella.

Her mother's all cross, pulls her away from the puddle

and says, 'Are you going to be here long? I've got to go and see my social worker woman. Can I leave her with you for half an hour? She likes you. She won't be any bother.' I said, 'Why can't she go with you?' She said, 'Because her dad'll be there and if he sees her he'll want to keep her. Go on.'

I was going to say no, only I didn't have to because just then Mr Parlane appears and wants a word so they clear off, leaving me with my arm still down the drain. I suddenly feel the culprit and it's two or three condoms all mixed up with leaves plugging up the pipe so I pull the lot out and all the dammed up water just empties away.

'Success,' I say to Mr Parlane and show him the bundle, 'Problem solved.' He said, 'No, not entirely. Would you step along to the office for a minute or two. And bring your barrow.'

It was Trickett who gave me my cards, with one week's pay in lieu, said I'd made several false statements so I'd better not have any silly ideas about wrongful dismissal and had I thought about bringing the Parks Department into disrepute let alone anything else.

Parlane hung about outside and when I came out said what about working in an old people's home or even a mortuary, somewhere out of harm's way, where I couldn't do any damage. 'Because you're a good worker, Wilfred, you really are.'

I went out the playground way, empty with it being wet, just a woman and a baby. I think she's a child minder. Only suddenly Samantha comes running out from behind the see-saw and gets hold of my hand. I said, 'Where's her mother?' The woman said, 'Gone over to the social. She said she'd be back by now. I've got to go, can I leave her with you?' I said, 'No.' 'Debbie said I could. She'll be back any minute. Let her go on the slide. She likes the slide.'

She wouldn't go on the slide because it was all wet, so we went and sat in the shelter. I put my hand on my knee and she put hers on top of it, then I put mine on and she topped it off with her hand. And we played that game for a bit. Sandwiches she called it.

Then I pretended to go to sleep, only she got on the seat and tried to open my eyes with her little fingers. She kept wanting to hold my hand but I wouldn't. Her little hand kept pecking at my hand, like a little bird trying to get in. Only my hand was a fist, honestly. Tight, she couldn't get in.

'There's nothing in there for you,' I said, 'I don't have anything for little girls. My shop's closed.' 'No it's not,' she says and slips her little finger in between my fingers and wiggles it about and looks at me and laughs.

She laughs again. She knew what she was doing. She must have known what she was doing.

So I took her in the bushes.

FADE.

White tiles. Wilfred is in prison clothes; eye swollen; bandage on his hand.

I said, 'She wanted to show me her dance.' Her mother said, 'What dance? She doesn't have a dance.' Somebody shouts out, 'You'll dance.'

They fetched me in and out the back way under a blanket. Women there shouting. Something hit me on the head. Said in the van it was a packet of cornflakes. Coins as well. Aught they have in their shopping bags.

They have to ravel it all out in words. 'Then what did you

do? Then what?' As if there was a plan. As if I meant to go from A to B. 'Well,' says the counsel, 'you bought the sweets, didn't you? You gave the wrong name.' I said to the young policewoman, 'It's what I thought she wanted.' 'That's what men always say,' she said, 'choose how old you are.'

Perhaps it would be easier, said the judge, if Samantha came up here. So she went and stood by his knee and held his hand. I thought, 'Well, that's what I'm here for.'

I asked for a number of other offences to be taken into consideration, some of them in Huddersfield where I've never even been. The police said it didn't matter as it meant they could close the book on lots of cases and it would go in my favour. It didn't. They just said my record proved that I was a hopeless case.

The judge said I would be given treatment. I haven't been given any treatment. They've put me by myself to stop the others giving me the treatment. The getting scalded in the kitchen treatment. The piss in your porridge treatment.

The doctor said, 'Did anyone touch you when you were little?' I said I didn't want any of that stuff. 'No, they didn't. And if they did, it's done. Anyway, they tell you to touch people now. They run courses in it.' 'Not like that,' he said.

Janet's been. Usual tack. Blames the mothers, says if they can't look after them they don't deserve kiddies in the first place. All her daffodils have been rooted up, plant pots broken. Next stop Newcastle, probably.

Mr Kumar. Says, I miss you Mr Paterson. I miss our walks with our barrows and brushes. You are the untouchable now. And he pats my hand. Says he's gone up one rung on the ladder now, is an attendant at the Art Gallery. 'No condoms to speak of,' he says. 'No sick on the floor. And on the walls the beautiful ladies and landscapes of Leeds. I tell you, Mr Paterson, it is a cushy number.'

When they put me away last time I used to think when I got out I'd go somewhere right away, a shed in the middle of a moor. And I'd fence it round with railway sleepers and get myself a bad dog and be a recluse.

Only kids would come. They'd know.

The prison must be near the station. I hear the trains on a night. And a school somewhere. There's a playtime at a quarter to eleven. And they come out at four. It's the one bit of my life that feels right and it's that bit that's wrong.

Men groan and cry out. Shout and scream in the night. It's like a tropical forest. Wild beasts.

I didn't foist them off like grown-ups do. I looked at them. I listened to them.

Sometimes there's a plane crosses the top left hand corner of my window. I think of the 'No Smoking' sign going on, the seats put back in the upright position, the pilot beginning his descent to Leeds and Bradford airport.

I used to go hiking when I was a boy. Over Nidderdale Moors. A reservoir. That would be the place. Nobody there at all.

FADE, *and in the black a long drawn-out howl.*

THE OUTSIDE DOG

Marjory · Julie Walters

AFTERNOON. THE KITCHEN. AGAINST A BLANK, WALLPAPERED WALL. ONE CHAIR. POSSIBLY SOME ARTIFICIAL FLOWERS. SIMILAR SETTINGS THROUGHOUT.

I'd be the same if it was a cat. Because they make as much mess as dogs. Only cats you can be allergic to, so people make allowances. And flowers, of course, some people. Only we don't have flowers. Well, we do but they're all washable. I just think it spies on me, that tongue lolling out.

He took the van over to Rawdon last night. Said it was Rawdon anyway. Doing something or other, fly-tipping probably. Takes Tina which was a relief from the woof-woofing plus it gave me a chance to swill.

I'd had Mrs Catchpole opposite banging on the door in the afternoon saying she was going to the council because it wanted putting down. I said, 'I agree.' She said, 'I'm getting a petition up.' I said, 'Well, when you do, fetch it across because I'll be the first signatory.' I hate the flaming dog. Of course she doesn't do it with him. Never makes a muff when he's around.

He comes in after midnight, puts his clothes in the washer. I said to him last week, 'Why don't you do your washing at a cultivated hour?' He said, 'You're lucky I do it at all.' Still, at least the washer's in the shed. I shouted down, 'That dog's not inside is she?' He said, 'No. Get to sleep.' Which I was doing only when he comes up he has nothing on. He leaves it a bit then slides over to my side and starts carrying on.

Found a dog hair or two on the carpet this morning so that meant another shampooing job. I only did it last week. This shampoo's got air-freshener in, plus a disinfectant apparently.

Non-stop down at the yard since they started killing off

the cows, so when he comes in this dinner-time he wants to eat straight off. Swills his boots under the outside tap and he's coming in like that. I said, 'Stuart. You know the rules. Take them off.' He said, 'There's no time.' So I said, 'Well, if there's not time you'll have it on the step.' Sits there eating and feeding Tina. She licks his boots. Literally. I suppose it's with him coming straight from the slaughterhouse.

Seems to have lost another anorak, this one fur-lined.

FADE.

She comes up this afternoon, his mother, all dolled up. Says, 'You've got this place nice. How do you manage with our Stuart?' I said, 'I've got him trained.' She said 'He's not trained when he comes down our house.' 'Well,' I said, 'perhaps he doesn't get the encouragement.' She said, 'I don't like it when they're too tidy. It's not natural.'

Not natural at their house. They've no culture at all. First time I went down there they were having their dinner and there was a pan stuck on the table. When it comes to evolution they're scarcely above pig-sty level. And she must be sixty, still dyes her hair, fag in her mouth, big ear-rings. She said, 'You don't mind if I smoke? Or do you want me to sit on the step?'

I gave her a saucer only it didn't do much good, ash all over the shop. She does it on purpose. It had gone five, she said, 'Where is he?' I said, 'Where he generally is at this time of day: slitting some defenceless creature's throat. They're on overtime.'

She went before it got dark. Said she was nervous what with this feller on the loose. Made a fuss of Tina. Remembered her when she was a puppy running round their house. I remember it an' all. Doing its business all up and down, the place stank. It was me that trained Stuart. Me that trained the dog.

Except for the din. Can't train that. Leaves off, of course when he appears. He doesn't believe she does it. I said to him, 'Is it safe for me to go on to the library?' He said, 'Why?' I said, 'There's a lass dead in Wakefield now.' He said, 'You don't cross any waste ground. Take Tina.'

Anyway I didn't go and when he's changed out of his muck and swilled everything off he put on his navy shirt, little chain round his neck and the tan slacks we bought him in Marbella. I brought him a beer in a glass while I had a sherry. Him sat on one side of the fire, me on the other, watching TV with the sound down. I said, 'This is a nice civilised evening.'

Except of course madam gets wind of the fact that we're having a nice time and starts whimpering and whatnot and jumping up outside the window and carries on and carries on until he has to take her out. Gone two hours so I was in bed when he got back.

Comes upstairs without his trousers on. I said, 'What've you done with your slacks?' He said, 'The dog jumped up and got mud on. Anyway it's quite handy isn't it?' I said, 'Why?' He said, 'Why do you think? Move up.'

Lots of shouting and whatnot. I thought in the middle of it, it's a blessing we're detached. 'Sorry about that,' he said when he'd done. 'I get carried away.'

Loudspeaker van came round this afternoon saying the police were going to be coming round. House to house. I was just getting some stuff ready to take to the dry cleaners while it was light still.

Couldn't find his slacks.

FADE.

She said, 'Have you any suspicions of anyone in your family?' I said, 'What family? There's only me and him.' He said, 'We can't talk with this dog carrying on. Can't we come inside?' I said, 'You've told people not to open their doors.' She said, 'But we're the police.' I said, 'Well, take your shoes off.'

She's in uniform, he's got a raincoat on. She said, 'We've had complaints about the dog. It's in your print-out.' I said, 'Oh it's the dog, is it? I thought it was the killer you were after.' She said, 'Your hubby says it never barks.' I said, 'When did you talk to him?' She said, 'At his place of employment. These are the dates of the murders. Look at them and tell me whether you can remember where your husband was on any of these dates.' I said, 'He was at home. He's always at home.' She said, 'Our information is he'll sometimes go out.' I said, 'Yes. With the dog. Do you know dogs? They occasionally want to have a jimmy riddle.' She said, 'What about this fly-tipping? His van's been seen.' I said, 'The van's not my province. Though I've shared the back seat with a beast head before now.'

Meanwhile the one in the raincoat's been sitting there saying nothing, looking round, sizing the place up. Suddenly he stands up. 'Can I use the toilet?' I said, 'Now? Well, you'll have to wait while I put a paper down.'

I took him upstairs and waited outside. He says, 'I can't do it with you listening.' So I came downstairs again. And she says, 'He's got a funny bladder.'

'One last question. Have you noticed anything out of the ordinary about your husband stroke boy friend stroke father stroke son...well, that's husband in your case...over the last six months?' 'Like what?' 'Blood on his clothes?' I said, 'There's always blood. He's a slaughterman. Only you won't find any in here. And you won't find any outside. He swills it off.' I said, 'Your friend's taking his time.' She said, 'Men have problems with their water. I've an idea he has an appliance.'

When eventually he comes down he says, 'You keep the place tidy.' I said, 'I used to be a teacher.' He said, 'What did you teach?' I said, 'Children.' He said, 'Do you have any?' I said, 'Does it look like it?'

As they're going Mother Catchpole opposite is stood in the road and shouts across, 'I've got something to tell you.' So the girl goes over and has a word. Comes back. 'Nothing,' she says. 'Just the flaming dog.' 'Nobody listens to me,' she's shouting, 'I've had a depression with that dog.'

I shut the door. When I went upstairs to wipe round the toilet I saw he'd moved one or two ornaments. Nothing else that I could see.

When his lordship came in I said, 'You never told me they'd been to your work.' He said, 'It was routine. I've tipped on one of the sites where they found one of them.' I said, 'Did you find that ticket?' He said, 'What ticket?' 'For the dry cleaners. The tan slacks.' He said, 'Oh yes. They're at work.' I said, 'You're not wearing them for work. They're good slacks are them.' He said, 'They're shit-coloured. What do I want with shit-coloured trousers?'

He was in the yard swilling his boots when he was saying all this. Outside. He's started being much more careful about all that. I don't know what's got into him.

FADE.

Lad opposite just delivering four pizzas to No. 17. She's a

widow, living on her own with a son in New Zealand and a heart condition, what's she wanting with four pizzas? I bet she's never had a pizza in her life. They must think I'm stupid. The doctor said, 'Why can't you sleep?' I said, 'The police are bugging my home.' She said, 'Yes. There's a lot of it about.' Asian too. They're normally a bit more civil.

We went out in the van the other night and he stopped it somewhere and said, 'Do you think it's me?' I said, 'No.' He said, 'Well, my mam does. It was her that went to the police.' 'And what did they say?' 'Told her she wasn't the only one. Mothers queuing up apparently.' I said, 'Well, she might cut a bit more ice if she didn't wear that leopard-skin coat thing. Legacy from when she was at it herself.' 'At what?' 'Soliciting.' He said, 'Who told you that?' I said, 'You did. You said she was hard up.' He said, 'It was years ago. I was still at school.'

Went out with Tina later on and comes in all worked up again. Sets to. Thought he was going to go through the bed. And saying stuff out loud again. I thought of them across the road, listening, so I put my hand over his mouth at one point, which he seemed to like.

I waited to see if there was anything in the papers only there wasn't. Been nothing for about a week now. You can get things out of proportion, I think.

I found where they'd put their listening thing this morning. Little hole in the skirting board. Did it when he was reckoning to go to the lavatory. Must have been quick because he'd managed to colour it white so it didn't show only some fluff got stuck to the paint so that's how I spotted it.

Sound of a newspaper coming through the door.
She picks it up.

They've found another one, it looks like. This time on a skip. Been there...about a week.

FADE.

One of them leaps over the wall, quite unnecessarily in my opinion because the gate's wide open. They get it off the TV. Five police cars. Batter on the door and when he opens it bowl him over and put handcuffs on him and take him off with a jacket over his head.

Tina, of course is going mad and they've got a dog of their own which doesn't help. I said, 'You're not fetching that thing in here.' He said, 'We've got a warrant.' I said, 'His dog's not been in here so I don't see why your dog should.' He said, 'This is an instrument of law enforcement.' I said, 'Yes, and it's an instrument of urinating against lampposts and leaving parcels on pavements. I don't want it sniffing round my stuff.' He says, 'You've got no choice, love,' and shoves me out of the way.

One of them's upstairs going through the airing cupboard. I said, 'What are you looking for? Maybe I can help?' He said, 'If you must know we're looking for the murder weapon.' I said, 'Oh, I can show you that. This is the murder weapon (*Points to her tongue*). This is always the murder weapon. You want to drag the canal for that.'

He said, 'You sound sicker than he does. I don't think you realise the seriousness of your situation. If we find you know what's been going on you'll be in the dock yourself.' I said, 'Don't put those sheets back. I shall have them all to wash now you've been handling them.' He said, 'We shall want all his clothes and other selected items,' and produces a roll of bin bags. 'Is everything here? He hasn't got anything at the dry cleaners?' I said, 'No.' I said, 'How do I know we'll get all this stuff back?' He said, 'That's the least of your worries.'

When eventually they go the handler reckons to take charge of Tina, except that he can't get her to go in the car with them. Then when they do force her in they all pile out sharpish because she's straightaway done her business in the car. I laughed.

It was suddenly quiet when they'd gone, just Mother Catchpole at her gate shouting. 'The doctor says I'm clinically depressed. That dog wants putting down.'

The police said not to touch anything but I wasn't having the place left upset like that so I set to and cleaned down and repaired the ravages a bit. One or two folks outside the house looking in and the phone rings now and again but I don't answer.

Dark by the time I'd finished but I didn't turn the lights on, just sat there. They must have charged him around six because suddenly there's cars drawing up and the phone's going like mad and reporters banging on the door and shouting through the letter-box and whatnot.

I just sit there in the dark and don't take on.

FADE.

Another parcel of excrement through the letter-box this morning. Postmarked Selby. Pleasant place. We had a little run there once in the van. Saw the cathedral, abbey, whatever it is. Shop with booklets and teatowels the way they do. Had a cup of coffee at a café down a street. The postman whanged it through that hard it split on the doormat.

It's probably deliberate. I'd got some plastic down from the previous times but still I'd to set to again. Spend a fortune on Dettol.

The trial's in Manchester for some reason. Out of the area. They can't call me unless I choose. Which I don't. Woman spat at me in Sainsbury's so I shop at the Asian shops now. Everywhere else they stare. Have to go thirty miles to get a perm. Go by minicab. Asians again. Never liked them much before. Don't ask questions. Godsend.

Reporter comes ringing the doorbell this afternoon. I think they must take it in turns. Shouts through the letter-box. I said, 'You want to be careful with that letter-box. You don't know what's been through it.' Says I'm sitting on a gold mine. Talks about £10,000. My side of the story.

Final speeches today. It rests on the dog, apparently, the rest is circumstantial. The van seen where the murders were, stopped once even but nothing else. Nothing on his tools. Nothing on his clothes. Only they found some blood belonging to the last one on the dog. The defence says it could have rolled in the blood because with the dog being fastened up all day when they went off he let it roam all over. So it doesn't mean he was with her, or anywhere near as the dog was off the lead.

The judge likes dogs. Has a dog of his own apparently. I don't know that'll make any difference.

I saw him before the trial started. Looked thinner. I was disappointed not to see him wearing a tie. I thought a tie would have made a good impression only they use them to commit suicide apparently.

I wish I'd something to do. I've cleaned down twice already. The yard wants doing only I can't do it with folks and reporters hanging about.

PAUSE.

He's lying, of course. Our Tina hasn't been seen to, so when he takes her out he never lets her off the lead. Ever.

FADE.

'Marjory! Marjory!'

They still shout over the gate now and again, one of them there this morning. Most of them have gone only they leave a couple of young ones here just in case I go shopping. Jury's been out two days now and they think it might be a week.

Anyway I thought while the heat was off I might be able to sneak out into the yard and give the kennel a good going over. The forensics took away her blanket so that's a blessing. I said to the feller, 'Don't bother to fetch it back. I'd have wuthered it long since if he'd let me.'

I peeped out of the gate to see if it's safe to swill and there's just a couple of the young reporters sat on Mrs C's doorstep having a cup of tea. I don't know what she's going to do when it's all over. She's had the time of her life.

Anyway I chucked a bucket of water under the kennel and then another only it didn't seem to be coming out the other side. I thought it was muck that had built up or something so I went in and got a wire coat hanger and started scraping about underneath and there's something there.

It was his tan slacks, all mucky and plastered up with something. I sneaked in and got a bin bag and fetched them inside.

Thinking back the police had been round with the dog but I suppose it couldn't smell anything except Tina. I sit there staring at this bag wondering whether there's anybody I should ring up. Suddenly there's a banging at the door and a voice through the letter-box.

'Marjory! Marjory!'

I didn't listen I ran with the bag and put it in the cupboard under the stairs. More clattering at the door.

'Marjory! Marjory! They've come back, the jury. He's been acquitted. He's got off. Can we have a picture?'

FADE.

The young woman says, 'Did I want any assistance with costume or styling? There'll be a lot of photographers.' I said, 'What's the matter with what I've got on?' She said, 'I could arrange for someone to come round and give you a shampoo and set.' I said, 'Yes, I could arrange for someone to come round and give you a kick up the arse.'

Though come to think of it I couldn't actually. She said, 'The paper's got a lot of money invested in you.' I said, 'Well, that's your funeral.'

Picture of him and the dog on the front page this morning, dog licking his face, ears up, paws on his shoulder, loving every minute of it. Spent the night in a hotel, five star, paid for by the newspaper. Article 'These nightmare months.' I stood by him, apparently. Says the longed-for reunion with his wife Marjory is scheduled for sometime this afternoon.

Police furious. The inspector in charge of the investigation said, 'Put it this way. We are not looking for anybody else.'

Sat waiting all afternoon. Photographers standing on the wall opposite, and on chairs and kitchen stools, two of them on top of a car. One up a tree. Police keeping the crowds back.

Getting dark when a big car draws up. Pandemonium.

Policeman bangs on the door, and Stuart's stood there on the doorstep and all the cameras going and them shouting, 'Stuart, Marjory. Over here. Over here please.' They want pictures of us with the dog, only the fellow from the newspaper says, No. They're going to be exclusive, apparently.

I said, 'Well, I've washed her kennel.' He says, 'She's not staying in there.' I said, 'You're not fetching her inside.' He said, 'I bloody am.' I said, 'Well, she'll have to stay on her paper.'

Later on when we're going to bed I wanted to shut her downstairs in the kitchen but he wouldn't have that either, keeps kissing her and whatnot and says she has to come upstairs.

When we're in bed he starts on straightaway and keeps asking Tina if she's taking it all in.

Afterwards he said, 'Are you surprised I'm not guilty?' I said, 'I'm surprised you got off.' He said, 'Don't you think I'm not guilty?' I said, 'I don't know, do I?' He said, 'You bloody do. You'd better bloody know. You're as bad as my mam.' I said, 'I'm not your mam.' He said, 'No, you're bloody not' and laughs.

I must have fallen asleep because when I wake up he's sleeping and the dog's off its paper, sat on his side of the bed watching him.

I get up and go downstairs and get the bin bag from under the stairs only I don't put any lights on. Then I get the poker and go out into the yard and push the slacks back under the kennel.

It's a bit moonlight and when I look over the gate they've all gone, just a broken chair on the pavement opposite.

I get back into bed and in a bit he wakes up and he has another go.

FADE.

NIGHTS IN THE GARDENS OF SPAIN

Rosemary · Penelope Wilton

A PLAIN SUBURBAN DRAWING ROOM WALL. ROSEMARY IS A MIDDLE-AGED, MIDDLE-CLASS WOMAN, SITTING ON A CHAIR.

Nobody normally gets killed round here; they're mostly detached houses and you never even hear shouting. So it took me a minute to tipple to what she was saying.

I said, 'Dead? Is it a heart attack?' She said, 'Oh no. Nothing like that. Just look at me, I'm in my bare feet.'

I really only know her to nod to but they have a lovely magnolia so once when she was in the garden I called out, 'You've had more luck with your magnolia grandiflora than I have.' But she just smiled and said, 'Yes.' And since I didn't have another remark up my sleeve ready, that was the end of that. I do that all the time, start a conversation but can't keep it going.

Blondish woman, a bit washed-out looking. Nice, tired sort of face. Anyway she comes out into the road and waits for me to get to their gate and says, 'I know I don't really know you, only there's something wrong with Mr McCorquodale.'

I was actually rushing because I'd planned on getting the five to nine and going into Sainsbury's but anyway I went in. I said, 'Has he been poorly?' She said, 'No. I've a feeling he's dead. Come through...only Mrs Horrocks...he doesn't have any trousers on.' I said, 'Well, I do a stint at the hospice twice a week, that's not a problem.' Only to be fair I just take the trolley round I've never actually been there when anybody's been going and they think I'm not really ready to administer the consolation yet.

She had a nice linen dress on, very simple. I think she might have been drinking.

He was lying on his back on the rug, one of those fleecy

hairy things with blood and whatnot coming from somewhere behind his head. And it's awful because the first thing I thought was, Well, she'll never get that out.

He had on these green Y-fronty things which I'd have thought were a bit young for someone who's retired, but Henry's the same, suddenly takes it into his head to go in for something he thinks is a bit more dashing. Little Terylene socks. I said, 'Should I touch him?' She said, 'Well, you can if you want but he is dead. I've been sitting here looking at him for an hour.' I said, 'His pants are on back to front.' She said, 'Oh that's me. I thought I'd better put them on before I fetched somebody in.'

He had a little tattoo not far from his belly button and I remember when they moved in Henry said he thought he had something to do with vending machines.

I said, 'Did he bang his head, do you think?' She said, 'Oh no. I shot him. I've put the gun away.' And she opens the sideboard drawer and there it is with the tablemats and playing cards. He had a gun because he'd been in Malaya apparently.

My first thought was to ring Henry and ask what to do but I couldn't face the fuss. I was still a bit nervous of calling 999 because I'm never sure what constitutes an emergency. Anyway I thought if she'd waited an hour already I might as well get her a cup of tea first, and as I was running the tap I called out, 'The police haven't already been, have they?' She said, 'No. Why?' I said, 'Nothing.'

Only there was a pair of handcuffs on the draining board.

FADE.

Another wall.

The policeman had some difficulty writing. Big boy, nice ears, spelling all over the place.

When I asked him what he thought had happened he said, 'Well, it's marriage isn't it, the stresses and strains of. Though we don't normally expect it with oldish people, they've generally got it out of their system by then. And it's a bit early in the day. People seem to like to get breakfast out of the way before the shooting starts.'

I'm just signing my statement when Henry arrives back and of course prolongs the process. 'I don't know that Mrs Horrocks quite means this, officer. What you said to me on the phone, young lady was…' I said, 'Henry. You weren't there.' The policeman winks and says, 'Now then, we don't want another shooting match do we?'

I mean at first Henry didn't even know who they were. He said, 'Not the chow?' I said, 'No. That's the Broadbents.' Anyway he sits about for a bit, whistling under his breath, then goes upstairs and attacks his computer.

After the policeman had gone I went up and apologised and asked Henry whether he thought anything had been going on. He said, 'Why?' I said, 'Well, she didn't have anything on under that linen dress.' Of course any suggestion of that embarrasses Henry, he's such an innocent. He said, 'Rosemary, I don't know what sort of world you think you're living in but there's probably some perfectly reasonable explanation. In the meantime let's just remember that somebody has died. I'm only sorry that you had to be the one who was passing, because I'd have preferred you not to have been involved.'

I went out later to get some milk at the garage and there were still one or two reporters outside number 17, a whole branch of the magnolia broken off. One of them said, 'Are you a neighbour? Did you know the McCorquodales?' I shook my head and didn't say anything so one of them shouts after me, 'You owe it to the community.' So I turned round and said, 'Yes, and you owe it to the community not to break branches off people's magnolia trees.' And of course that's just the point where the photographer takes a picture and it's in the paper this morning with me looking like a mad woman and the caption 'The real face of suburbia.' Whereas the real face of suburbia was Henry's when he saw it.

I woke up in the night and I could hear him whistling under his breath. I said, 'Are you thinking about Mrs McCorquodale?' He said, 'No, I was thinking about the house. Prices are down as it is and something like this isn't going to help matters.' He reached over from his bed and took my hand. 'You must try not to be upset, but if we don't get at least 175 we shall have to kiss goodbye to Marbella.'

I keep wondering if I ought to have told somebody about the handcuffs.

FADE.

Rosemary is in the conservatory.

I'd put on my little greeny-coloured costume, which is at least tried and tested, only when I came down Henry said, 'Oh, are you going in that?' So I went and changed into the black. No need, because it was all very casual, the policeman in his shirt sleeves, and some barrister taking me through what I'd said, scarcely interested at all. I gave her a little smile; they let her sit down most of the time, she did look pale.

Pleaded not guilty, which you have to do apparently even

when they know you did it, only then her lawyer reads out a list of stuff they'd found wrong with Mrs McCorquodale when she'd been arrested, old fractures, new cigarette burns and one of her teeth loose. Another lawyer then jumps up and said, 'Were other people involved?' And she said, 'No,' and he said he wouldn't pursue that at this stage. The upshot is she was sent for trial.

I said to Henry, 'Does that mean they'll have to go through it all again?' He said, 'Oh yes. This is just the beginning.'

Policewoman came round this afternoon, said Did I want any counselling? I'm entitled to it, apparently, through having seen a body and should have had it earlier only they had a charabanc run off the road so they've had a bit of a backlog.

Pleasant enough girl, though she would go on about all the terrible dreadful things she'd seen, accidents and violence and whatnot, so my seeing just one body seemed pretty ordinary really. But maybe that's part of the counselling. We sat in the garden having some tea. Heavy on the biscuits; polished off half a dozen sandwich creams. She said, It was nice it was so civilised, had I seen a naked corpse before?

She was just going when she turns back and she says, 'Mrs Horrocks, when I went on the counselling course one of the things they teach you is that it helps to look things in the face right from the start.' I said, 'Well, I did look at the body; I actually touched it.' She said, 'Yes, but when the police start digging, which they have to do, there is a potential for distress.' I said, 'Digging?' She said, 'Metaphorically.' I said, 'Why should it affect me?' She said, 'All the indications are that it won't. But the potential is there. Things come out and I want you to know I'm here for you. I'm on a bleep.'

I said to Henry, 'It's nice she should be so concerned.'

He said, 'It's what she's there for...unfortunately.'

Article in the *Mail* yesterday, which I'd always thought was that bit more refined but it's full of silly stuff about the case, what goes on behind the neat privet hedges-type-thing. I said to Henry, Fat lot they know. There actually isn't a privet hedge in the entire road. They're mostly beech and one or two cypresses leylandii. He said he didn't think that was quite the point and to a reporter a hedge was simply something to be peered through.

Still, talking of neat, what with her being away on remand their garden which is usually so immaculate is already beginning to look a bit... well...shaggy. She's got a herb garden outside the back door and the borage has gone berserk, bullying its way all over the border. Made me long to nip over and put it in its place.

I didn't want to ask Henry, though, as I was sure he'd think it 'Inadvisable, Rosemary, quite candidly,' but no, it turns out he's all in favour and it had in fact occurred to him, though, it has to be said, coming at it from a different angle from me, saying that if ever we're going to get anywhere near our asking price a garden going to seed in the same road is the last thing one wants.

So the upshot is I've started toddling up the road with my trusty secateurs. Thought I'd cut back the poppies now that they've flowered and give the achillea a chance to come through. Of course, I've scarcely got my kneeling pad down before Miss Lumsden's out, contriving to come by with an unconvincing bottle of Lucozade en route for the bottle bank. Wants to know if there are any sweet peas going begging. I said I'd thought of picking some and taking them down to the hospice. She said 'What a nice idea. Some people might feel a bit funny about them but I suppose they're too far gone to care.'

And lots of jokes of course. On the lines of Mr Pemberton's 'Who do I have to shoot for you to come and do my garden?' Smile got a bit fixed after a bit. Except that Sheila Blanchard did actually come in and lend a hand weeding the borders. Said she didn't blame her a bit. 'I mean husbands, Rosemary. Who needs them?' I said, 'Well, they can be a comfort.' She said, 'Can they? Reggie isn't. I'm the comfort merchant. What's Henry like?' 'Oh,' I said 'very...' and I said such a silly word 'very considerate.' I saw her smile and she's a nice woman but I know it'll be all up and down the road by tomorrow.

But he is considerate. Timid, I suppose. Always has been. Wish he wasn't sometimes.

What I haven't told Henry is that I dropped Mrs McCorquodale a note to the prison, bringing her up to date on what I've been doing. I do it every day now, in fact, even send her snaps. Told her today I was keeping an eye on the alchemilla mollis, lovely plant but you have to read it the riot act occasionally.

She rang this afternoon to thank me. I didn't know you could do that in prison, ring up. Her name's Fran.

'Dear Fran...'

FADE.

The conservatory.

I've misjudged Henry. Got him quite wrong. Thirty years of marriage and you think you've got somebody all weighed up but no. He's lost half a stone while the case has been going on – and never set foot in the office. I thought, well, you're a better person than ever I thought you were. I said to Fran, 'He's more worried about you than he's ever been about me.' I mean the day I had my scan he went off to a golf tournament.

So as a reward I got out the brochures for Marbella and that seemed to cheer him up.

It's all come out in court, though. Turns out that Mr has led her a dog's life. Literally. The defence produced the collar and lead in evidence. Beat her. Terrorised her. 'A saga of protracted and imaginative cruelty' counsel said.

The prosecution, of course, goes after her, claiming it was all part of some game, sexually speaking, and that the cruelty was what she wanted. But she said if it had been mutual he wouldn't have been interested. Anyway how is it mutual to have your arm broken?

A lot of lurid details, how he sometimes used to put a hood over her head so's she couldn't see and bring in other people to watch. Business associates, she thought. Leading lights in the world of vending machines, probably.

Henry says she was lucky because there was another case going on the same week up in Liverpool, a man had up for killing a child, and that pushed her out of the limelight a bit.

Of course, what Henry calls the wild and woolly feminist ladies were out in force even shouting from the gallery. 'To a degree irresponsible,' Henry said. 'However mitigating the circumstances, Rosemary, she has to be looking at a custodial sentence.' Then, when he only gave her two years, the judge gets it in the neck from the law and order brigade. But, as Sheila Blanchard said, 'Worth every minute of it, dear, if you ask me. A couple of years basket weaving and you get the bed to yourself. Cheap at the price. I just wish I had a gun. As it is I'm pinning my hopes on his prostate.'

I can't go and see her so often now she's convicted and Henry doesn't know I go at all. Well, I've never had a best friend, the sort you can tell everything to. Never had one, never been one, even when I was a girl. Not the type, I suppose. And no secrets to tell either. And with not having children I wasn't a member of that club either.

She's in Rissington, the other side of York. It's one of these modern places, looks like a business park or an out of town shopping centre. Crimes 'R' Us. She's transformed the prison garden, which used to be very utilitarian, cabbages, lettuces and whatnot.

Only now she's got them to do some interplanting, even make it a bit of a potager...and while it's never going to be Sissinghurst...the site's too windy...it's still streets ahead of what it was. She has visions of it being open to the public but that's difficult with it being a prison. We go and sit on a seat in the garden and she's started telling me about all the stuff he forced her to do. Said she wanted me to know in case it made me not want to see her any more. I said, 'Don't be silly.' But terrible things I never knew people did. And with the hood over her head and men there, watching in silence. More than watching actually.

One of them who had a funny habit...and I knew what she was going to say the second before she said it...a funny habit of whistling under his breath.

Pause.

Of course, a lot of people do that.

FADE.

Kitchen.

'I see they're selling the Murder House,' Sheila Blanchard calls out to me this morning. 'The board's gone up. Asking 160.' I didn't say I knew, or that actually it's sold already. Fran says they're an Asian family, quite well-to-do, have a chain of electrical shops. I thought, Well, that won't do Marbella any good. Poor Henry. Golf with Jimmy Tarbuck takes a knock.

I look at him a lot now, this once upon a time spectator, or maybe still, who knows, somewhere. And I think... Well, sometimes I just think, 'You dark horse.' Other times I think about Fran and get upset. He caught me staring at him the other night, said 'What are you looking at, young lady?' I said, predictably, 'Nothing.' 'You've been getting a bit broody lately,' he said. And he patted me on the knee. (*She pulls a face.*)

What I'd actually been thinking was whether all these years he'd been wanting to see me crawl round the room naked on my hands and knees. No worse than bedding out, I suppose, though if I did it nowadays I'd have to have my knee pads on, which might take the edge off things a bit.

But I think about the collar and lead, then I think Well, that's what my marriage has been like too, being jerked along. I mean, what else is Marbella?

We never settled on what to call it, that was part of the trouble. The garden's made me quite used to things having a common name and a Latin one. Only with sex neither seemed to suit Henry. Coming from me, anyway. Just got embarrassed.

He's no idea I go and see her. I tell him it's the hospice. The farm goes from strength to strength; she's put her onions in for shows and gone commercial with the tomatoes. She's there every free moment, well, I say free. Except that when I say goodbye at the gate it feels it's me that's going back to prison.

Once a month they let her out for a half day and we go off for the afternoon and do all sorts. Open gardens, obviously, auctions we've been to, car boot sales. And old churches, which I've never cared much for, only Fran knows a lot about them. One church in the middle of a field near where there'd been a battle. And we sit there in a pew while she explains all the architectural features. And sometimes I think I've never been so happy in my life.

She took my arm this last time, just as we were coming down some steps at Fountains Abbey and then, when we got to the bottom, she didn't let go. It was just like it was when I was a girl when a boy did it. Such a bold step. And so meant.

And I thought, here I am strolling arm in arm with someone who murdered her husband. I said…out loud… 'I know what this is.' She said, 'What is it?' I said, 'It's life.'

She wasn't feeling all that clever today so we just went and sat in the grounds, and she held my hand again. Going into York next week for a check-up. I thought I could go along and hang about the hospital just on the off-chance I might see her but she'll be with a warder apparently so I won't.

Gave me this.

She has a large tomato which she puts to her cheek.

FADE.

A patio wall. A tropical night. Crickets, etc.

I've never had to start a garden from scratch before. There are no features at all. Flat, square, stony it's like one of the 'before' pictures in the gardening magazines. Or an exercise yard.

A lawn's pretty much out of the question in this heat and the water supply's very quixotic, though Henry says the greens at the golf club are immaculate. And he saw Sean Connery last week. So I sit and look at it and draw plans. 'Look on it as a challenge,' Henry says. 'You'll crack it, young lady,' he says. 'I know you.' (*The dialogue is now quite broken up.*)

She died, did Fran. A lot of toing and froing before they eventually tracked it down. No surprise to either of us. Doctors. It's the first thing that occurs to you and the last thing that occurs to them. By which time it's too late. 'Oh, it was always too late, Mrs Horrocks.'

She was in a hospice at the finish so I knew the drill. I used to hold her hand, kiss it. And she'd kiss mine. We'd talked about a little garden centre.

Best thing that could have happened, Henry said. Which is when I should have packed my bags. Instead of which I just went and sat in the greenhouse for a bit. Typical.

He'll sometimes wear one of these caps with the big peaks that boys wear. Reckons it's for the sun. Caught him the other day wearing it back to front. I suppose it's known as a new lease of life.

There are supposed to be lots of criminals round here. Bank robbers and such like who can't go back, play golf all day.

Of course it's just what would happen in a play. Fran shot him so she had to pay. Only this place is crawling with people who haven't paid. Unless you count just being here as paying.

The gardening books talk about the plants that are supposed to like shade. They say they prefer it.

I don't believe it. I don't believe anything likes shade. They do perfectly well in the shade, it's true. But give them even…(*and there's quite a long pause*) give them a bit of sun and suddenly they come into their own.

I sit here at night, listening to the frogs and the crickets, and Henry, whistling under his breath.

FADE.

WAITING FOR THE TELEGRAM

Violet · Thora Hird

THE SPEAKER IS AN OLD LADY IN A WHEELCHAIR. SHE HAS A RUG OVER HER KNEES. THE BACKGROUND IS PLAIN AND UNCLUTTERED. SOMETIMES SHE IS PARKED BY A RADIATOR, SOMETIMES BY A WINDOW OR THE END OF A BED. THE SHOTS NEED NOT BE CONTINUOUS AS WRITTEN BUT CAN BE BROKEN UP BY A CUTAWAY OF VIOLET'S HANDS, TWISTING HER HANDKERCHIEF, TURNING HER WEDDING-RING OR JUST FOLDED IN HER LAP. SOMETIMES WHEN SHE IS TRYING TO REMEMBER THINGS OR EXPRESS THEM SHE FILLS UP WITH TEARS BUT THESE ARE ONLY BRIEF AND SHE GENERALLY BATTLES ON.

I saw this feller's what-do-you-call-it today. Except I'm not supposed to say 'what-do-you-call-it'. Verity says, 'Violet. What-do-you-call-it is banned. When we cannot find the word we want we describe, we do not say 'what-do-you-call-it'. Well, you won't catch me describing that. Besides, 'what-do-you-call-it' is what I call it. Somebody's what-do-you-call-it. Anyway I saw it.

I didn't think anything about it only somebody must have gone and alerted the office because next thing you know Bouncing Betty poles in. She says, 'Violet, I have to ask you this. Was the penis erect?' I said, 'Nurse Bapty. That's not a word I would use.' She said, 'Erect?' I said, 'No. The other.' She said, 'Well, Violet. You've had what we call a stroke. You're sometimes funny with words.' I said, 'I'm not funny with that word.' She said, 'Things have changed now, Violet. Penis is its name. All the other names are just trying to make it more acceptable. Language is a weapon, Violet. We're at war.' I said, 'Who with?' She said, 'Men.'

He was a smartish feller, can't have been more than seventy and a lovely blue suit. He could have been a bank manager except he had no socks on. I said, 'You can put that away.' He said, 'I've got a big detached house in Harrogate.' I said, 'That's no excuse.' He said, 'It's got five bathrooms.'

She turns her wheelchair.

They've inaugurated this what-do-you-call (*She checks herself*) ...this chair-lift thing. I think he must have come up from downstairs. There's been one or two of them trying to migrate. They get bored. Do you wonder? Anyway when he saw it wasn't cutting much ice with me he takes it over to Hilda, only she's busy braying on her tray with her spoon so it doesn't make much of an impact there either. Mary's asleep and when he wakes her up and says, 'Look at this', she says, 'Is it dinner-time?' and goes back to sleep again.

In the finish he comes back to me and says, 'I've forgotten, did I show you this?' At which point Rene rushes in, sees his lordship with his trousers down and says, 'Are you my taxi? I'm all ready.'

I said to Francis, 'And they call it a rest home.'

FADE.

They haven't given it up. We were throwing this ball about... a big, felty thing...I could never catch a ball when I was little so I know I can't do it now. Anyway Nurse Bapty comes in and wheels me to the window and says, 'Violet, having seen this penis, would you like some counselling?' I said, 'Nurse. I'm nearly 95.' She said, 'Yes, Violet, but you're a victim and choose how old you are, you're still flying the flag of gender.' I said, 'Well I think a cup of tea would do the trick, Nurse Bapty, thank you.' I call them all Nurse and she is a nurse only a lot of them aren't, they're just young lasses.

Francis is a proper nurse, though, he's got letters after his name and you can tell because he has me out of my clothes in no time. I said, 'Somebody tried to undress me once, only he wasn't a patch on you. Are you as sharp as this with your girl friend?' He said, 'You're my girl friend.'

He has some grand arms.

FADE.

I can't reckon up names. New lass on this afternoon, bonny little thing, helping Francis put me to bed for my lie down. I said, 'What's your name, love?' She says, 'Devon.' I says, 'That's never a name, it's a place.' She says, 'Yes, a very beautiful place. My mam and dad used to go on holiday there.'

I said, 'Well, it's a good job they didn't go to Skegness.'

She looks right mad, only Francis laughs so she laughs an' all. I think she's got her eye on him.

I drop off and when I wake up there's a fellow by my bed. He goes, 'Hello!' I said, 'Hello' and shut my eyes again. They send these folks round to test you.

When I open them again he's still there. 'Hello!,' he goes. Fattish feller, sixty odd, gingery tash. He said, 'It's Donald, mother. I'm your son.'

He didn't look like a son, looked more like a father. Big wristwatch, attaché case, one of these green raincoaty-things they shoot in. Anyway I take no notice and he starts on the Hello! game again. Hello! Hello! Made me feel like a budgie. I said, 'Bugger off.'

Mrs...Mrs...light-coloured lady...Shah comes in, starts

squeegeeing round. He says, 'It's tragic, isn't it. She'd never had a day's illness in her life. I think it's a disease of civilisation. Does it happen in your country?' She says, 'I'm from Huddersfield.'

Then Rene comes in, ready for off as usual. She says, 'Are you my taxi? I've been waiting all morning.' 'I've just remembered,' he says, 'I'm wanted in Wakefield,' shoves his tash in my face and he's off. Mrs Shah says, 'Was that your son?' I said, 'He thinks so.' She says, 'My son's got in to do engineering. He's six foot two.'

I lay there working it out. If I had a son I must have had a...husband. So when Francis was wiping my bottom later on I said, 'Did I get married?' He said, 'Yes, can't you remember?' I said, 'I remember one young man but I don't think I took the plunge. Are you married?' He said, 'You get star treatment here, Violet. Even the Queen doesn't get her bottom wiped.'

FADE.

What's her name came round today...her that helps me with talking...(*She thinks*)...name of a cricket bat, else a gas oven... Verity. She's a nice-looking lass but makes nowt of herself, a big jumper thing...I said, I bet you've got a right nice...' She goes, 'Describe, Violet, describe...' I said, 'A right nice...them two things with pink ends that men like...Bust.'

By, she did look narked! She said, 'Things are different now, Violet. Women have control of their own bodies.' I said, 'Is that why I can't get them to take me to the toilet?'

Then we start doing these exercises, naming folks. I'm quite good at that...Rene, Mary, Hilda. And then I get stuck. She says, 'Describe, Violet. Say, the lady in the yellow frock.'

I said, 'The black lady.' She said, 'No, Violet. It's better to say the lady in the yellow frock.'

I says to Francis, 'It's a complicated business talking. I never used to give it a thought.' He said, 'What?'

He wasn't listening. He was miles away. Really quiet. Not like him. He's generally so full of...them things you get in tins...beans!

He's a lovely looking lad.

FADE.

Rene gollops her food. She was sick today all down Francis's front. I said, 'You gollop your food, you.' She said, 'Well, I have to. I've got a taxi coming.' I said, 'Rene, where's this taxi taking you?' She said, 'Armley.' I said, 'Armley where?' She said, 'My mam and dad's in 1947.' I said, 'Well, if he can take you there I bet he does a spanking trade.'

Anyway she fetches her dinner back all down Francis. So he says, 'You'll have to excuse me, ladies' and he takes his...tunicky thing...right off. And by, he's a grand-looking lad! Not a mark on him and right big (*She mimes shoulders*)...here. It made you want to...(*She mimes a kiss*)...do that, whatever it's called. Lovely. Devon came in I saw her having a look.

When he's finished cleaning up he says, 'Well, Violet you've seen something today.' I said, 'I've seen it before.' He just has a little bit of this (*She touches her hair*)... starting here (*She touches her chest*). Like they do at that age. (*She starts to cry.*) I said, 'Don't go get yourself...' He said, 'What?' I said, 'Like when you don't come back. Khaki...poppies.' He said, 'Nay, that's all done with now. They don't die like that.' And he looked right... (*She touches her cheeks meaning tears*)...what's it called?

FADE.

I saw my legs today. I didn't own them. They didn't look like my legs at all. That Devon was giving me a bath. I said, 'Them's never my legs.' She said, 'Whose legs do you think they are?' I said, 'Well, you never know in this place. I've had somebody else's teeth before now. And this frock isn't mine. Tangerine doesn't suit me. Where's that green little frock?' She said, 'Hilda kept wetting herself in it and it's gone funny.' Francis wouldn't have put me in this frock. Only he wasn't there.

She's putting me back on the bed and I said, 'Well I've learned one thing. I'm not Betty Grable.' She says, 'Who's she?' No wonder your talking goes...even when you get it right they think you're barmy. Francis knows all the old film stars...Betty Grable...her that sings and that one with the cig and her hair up...bit of a madam...Bette Davis.

Anyway I'm sitting up in bed when they all waltz in with this cake. Turns out it's my birthday. I'm ninety something... I don't know, they did tell me. Candles. Tasted like candles did the cake. Anyway I had to reckon to be... pleased (*She pretends to smile*)...Kept saying a few years more and I'll be getting the...now then...lad comes on a bike...folks stood at the door, weeping...telegram. Her on the horse at the end of the pictures, she sends it you apparently. Queen.

No Francis though. I said to Nurse Bapty, 'Where is he?' She said, 'He's gone for a check-up.' I said, 'Check-up for what?' She said, 'Oh, they do that now.'

Pause.

I hate tangerine.

FADE.

Verity fetches a young lad in this morning. She says to him, 'You're privileged. Violet is our oldest resident.' She says, 'Spencer's going to ask you one or two questions for his school project. It's about the past.'

Poor-looking lad, bonny face. Floppy clothes, shirt-tail out. I said, 'Is that your big brother's jumper?' He says, 'No. It's dead smart is this.' Gets out his exercise book, and says, 'What was it like then?' I said, 'Well...' He said, 'Were things better or worse?' I said, 'Well, my legs were better.' He said he didn't mean that. Verity comes back and he says, 'She doesn't seem to know what I'm talking about.' Verity says, 'Well, she's had a stroke. Come on, I'll find you another one.' (*Violet is a bit upset.*)

I said to Francis, 'He'd mean trams and whatnot. Strikes. Tin-baths. The war.' Francis says, 'Which war?' I said, 'The proper war when all the young lads got killed. "Never again." That war.' He looked right sad and said, 'Hold my hand.' So I did. Then he said, 'Did you have a young man?' I said, 'Yes.' He said, 'What was he like?' I said, 'His name was Edward. They had a little confectioner's down Tong Road. He used to fetch my mam a vanilla slice. Every time he came round, a vanilla slice.'

I still had hold of his hand. I said, 'When you were courting then, it was a kind of...where you fight...' He said, 'Struggle.' I said, 'Ay. He'd manage to get one button undone one night, and another the next. And lasses weren't supposed to do much in them days, just lie back and get ready to draw the line. And because I'd let him get so far one night, he'd know where the front line was, so the next night he'd get there a bit quicker and push on a bit further...another button, you know. It was that... grudging somehow. But it was the way you felt you had to be then.

Anyway he was going off to France next day; he was in camp over at Church Fenton and they'd given him a pass for his last night. My mam...oh she was a good 'un...she put some anemones in a vase...I love anemones... and put a fire in the front room and then she reckoned she had to stay at my Aunt Florence's that night. Ordinary folks then were better than they're ever given credit for, for all they were so straitlaced.

I gave him his tea and then we went and sat in the front room and he started on like, undoing my buttons and kissing and whatnot. Only I'd wanted to look nice so I'd put on my best frock and he couldn't fathom how it unfastened. I should just have taken it off but I didn't and, poor lamb, he got so fed up with these flaming buttons, in the finish he gave up.

He'd taken his leggings...his puttees off because they were hot and he was in his shirtsleeves; they were right rough khaki shirts then, really cheap and itchy. Anyway in the finish he gets up off the sofa and says, 'Hang this lot,' and he takes his shirt off and everything else besides. Doesn't say a word, just takes it all off and stands there on the hearthrug. Oh and he looked a picture, with the fire and that. Not a mark on him. Then he says, 'Take your clothes off now.'

She covers her face with her hands.

And I didn't. I didn't. And I wanted him so much. I don't know... it was just the way I'd been brought up. And he stands there looking down at me...and then he just picks his clothes up and goes next door and after a bit I heard the front door bang.

They look old in photographs compared with what they look now. Only they weren't. They were lads, same as you. And just as grand.

Pause.

I saw the yellow thing the boy on the bike brings...his sister fetches it round...telegram. And a vanilla slice for mam. Then later on they had a letter reckoning to be from the King, same as everybody did who'd lost somebody. They keep saying I'll be getting a telegram soon...for my birthday.'

Francis says, 'Do you know something Violet? In all that, you never said, "What do you call it?" or "What's its name?" Not once. You knew all the words.'

'Only I should have let him, shouldn't I? I've never forgiven myself.' 'Well,' Francis says, 'how can you know?' Still holding my hand.

Pause.

Poor lad, he looks right washed out.

FADE.

I thought they'd got pneumonia beat. A big strapping lad like Francis. Devon said it was a blessing, he'd have died anyway. I said, 'A blessing? A young feller like that?'

And he was such a gentle soul. She was doing my legs, plastering me up with stuff and right hard hands, not a patch on Francis. I said, 'He'd have made some lass a grand husband.' She said, 'It wasn't lasses; it was lads.' I said, I knew it was lads. She said, 'Well I wish you'd told me.' Right nasty.

Pause.

I didn't know it was lads but I wasn't having her telling me. Lads or lasses, he was a love.

Rene's gone an' all.

Violet looks towards the empty bed.

Went in the night. They thought I was asleep so they didn't bother to put the screens round. Saw it all. Putting the white socks on. Bit of giggling. Right as rain when she came to bed. Made me promise to wake her up if her taxi came. Well, it came in the finish. I said to Francis...no, I didn't.

Pause.

My arm seems to have gone to sleep this morning and this hand.

She looks at her hand.

Now then I'll have another one of these somewhere.

She locates her other hand, lifts it onto her lap and sits with her hands folded. She sings.

I've got sixpence
Jolly jolly sixpence
I've got sixpence
To last me all my life
I've got twopence to spend

And twopence to lend
And twopence to send home to my wife.
If we sang everything I shouldn't forget.

All this very broken up with pauses.

Pets is what you want in this place. Else babies. Summat you can…(*She makes a stroking movement*) do this with. Not have to talk to.

Pause.

It's no game is this.

Pause.

We're the pets. Fed and cleaned out every day. It's a kennels is this.

Pause.

Pedigree Chum. Pedigree Chum.

FADE.

ALAN BENNETT is one of Britain's best-loved and most highly acclaimed writers. He has written widely for radio, television and theatre. His latest play, *The History Boys*, won several awards, including *Evening Standard* and Critics' Circle Awards for Best Play and the Laurence Olivier Award for Best New Play. It also won six Tony Awards, including Best Play, following an extremely successful transfer to Broadway. In 2006 Bennett was named Author of the Year at the British Book Awards for *Untold Stories*, his recent collection of memoirs and diaries.

Also available from BBC Books

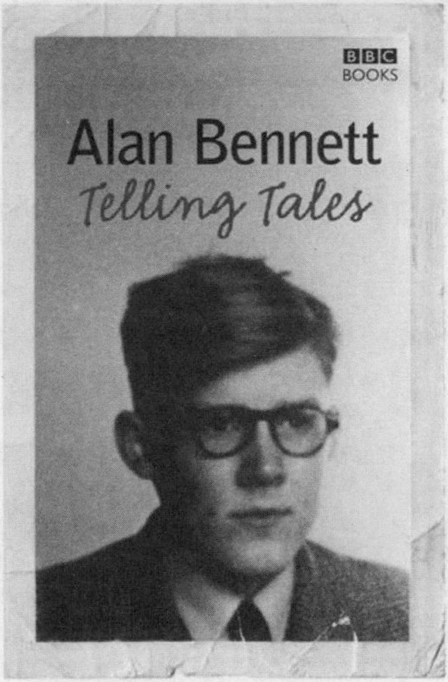